A LifeGuide® Bible Study

MATTHEW
Being Discipled by Jesus

**22 studies in two parts
for individuals or groups**

Stephen &
Jacalyn Eyre

With Notes for Leaders

IVP

InterVarsity Press
Downers Grove, Illinois

InterVarsity Press
P.O. Box 1400, Downers Grove, IL 60515
World Wide Web: www.ivpress.com
E-mail: mail@ivpress.com

InterVarsity Press® is the book-publishing division of InterVarsity Christian Fellowship/USA®, a student movement active on campus at hundreds of universities, colleges and schools of nursing in the United States of America, and a member movement of the International Fellowship of Evangelical Students. For information about local and regional activities, write Public Relations Dept., InterVarsity Christian Fellowship/USA, 6400 Schroeder Rd., P.O. Box 7895, Madison, WI 53707-7895.

Cover photograph: Dennis Flaherty

ISBN 0-8308-3003-0

Printed in the United States of America ∞

15	14	13	12	11	10	9	8	7	6	5	4	3	2
10	09	08	07	06	05	04	03	02	01				

Contents

GETTING THE MOST OUT OF *MATTHEW* ——————— 5

PART 1: DISCOVERING THE KING
MATTHEW 1:1—16:20

1 Matthew 1—2	**In Search of the King** ———	*9*
2 Matthew 3	**Preparing for the King** ———	*13*
3 Matthew 4	**The Beginning of the Kingdom** ———————	*16*
4 Matthew 5:1—6:18	**The Law of the King (Part 1)** ———————	*19*
5 Matthew 6:19—7:29	**The Law of the King (Part 2)** ———————	*23*
6 Matthew 8:1—9:34	**The Powers of the King** ——	*27*
7 Matthew 9:35—11:30	**The Messengers of the King** ———————	*30*
8 Matthew 12	**The Leaders & the King** ———	*33*
9 Matthew 13	**The Parables of the King** ———	*36*
10 Matthew 14	**The Revelation of the King** —	*39*
11 Matthew 15:1—16:20	**Understanding the King** ———	*42*

PART 2: THE REJECTION & RESURRECTION OF THE KING
MATTHEW 16:21—28:20

12 Matthew 16:21—17:27	**The Work of the King** ———	*45*

13 Matthew 18   **The Greatest in the Kingdom** ———— *50*

14 Matthew 19—20   **Life in the Kingdom** ———— *53*

15 Matthew 21:1-27   **The King Occupies His Capital** ———— *57*

16 Matthew 21:28—22:46   **The King Silences the Opposition** ———— *60*

17 Matthew 23   **The King Condemns the Rebels** ———— *63*

18 Matthew 24   **The Return of the King** ——— *66*

19 Matthew 25   **Preparation for the King's Return** ———— *69*

20 Matthew 26   **The Betrayal of the King** —— *72*

21 Matthew 27   **The Crucifixion of the King** ———— *76*

22 Matthew 28   **The Victory of the King** —— *80*

Leader's Notes ———————————— *84*

Getting the Most Out of *Matthew*

What does it mean to be a disciple of Jesus Christ? How can we effectively disciple others? Christian bookstores are full of "how to" manuals that seek to answer these questions. The early church had a discipling manual too—the book of Matthew. It was written to teach us how to be a disciple of Jesus Christ and how to disciple others. Before looking at current discipling manuals, why not go back to one of the originals?

Discipleship is the application of Christian truth to the present. "What does God want me to do about this relationship?" "How can I deal with anxiety?" We need to know what God expects of us on a daily basis. Discipleship is a very practical matter.

Practical questions were a concern of Matthew as he wrote his book. Matthew was a tax collector, so he knew how important it was to be practical. A tax collector has to know things like how much tax you owe, where you pay and who is authorized to collect it. And when a tax is paid, it must be recorded exactly. Otherwise government authorities tend to become hostile. Very practical stuff.

Matthew draws on all his background as he writes. Your most important need as a disciple is to know what the Lord is like. Matthew will help you. Through his work you will get to know Jesus better as he responds to needy people, handles conflict and faces opposition. You will also see Jesus as a king. How does he handle authority? What type of laws does he give? How does he provide for his subjects?

For your daily living you will discover how to handle anger and envy. You will learn how your faith can be strengthened, how to pray, how to grow in humility. You will gain insights into a biblical approach to evangelism. You will find out what attitudes the Lord thinks are important. And you will learn how to handle suffering and grief.

In short, a study of Matthew will help you become a better disciple and disciplemaker.

The content of Matthew will be covered by dividing it into two equal parts, 1:1—16:20 and 16:21—28:20. The first half is entitled "Discovering the King." It focuses on the identity and authority of Jesus. The second half is entitled "The Rejection & Resurrection of the King." It focuses on Jesus as he encounters opposition and persecution culminating in the cross and resurrection.

From beginning to end Matthew is an exciting and challenging Gospel. Get ready for an adventure!

Suggestions for Individual Study

1. As you begin each study, pray that God will speak to you through his Word.

2. Read the introduction to the study and respond to the personal reflection question or exercise. This is designed to help you focus on God and on the theme of the study.

3. Each study deals with a particular passage—so that you can delve into the author's meaning in that context. Read and reread the passage to be studied. If you are studying a book, it will be helpful to read through the entire book prior to the first study. The questions are written using the language of the New International Version, so you may wish to use that version of the Bible. The New Revised Standard Version is also recommended.

4. This is an inductive Bible study, designed to help you discover for yourself what Scripture is saying. The study includes three types of questions. *Observation* questions ask about the basic facts: who, what, when, where and how. *Interpretation* questions delve into the meaning of the passage. *Application* questions help you discover the implications of the text for growing in Christ. These three keys unlock the treasures of Scripture.

Write your answers to the questions in the spaces provided or in a personal journal. Writing can bring clarity and deeper understanding of yourself and of God's Word.

5. It might be good to have a Bible dictionary handy. Use it to look up any unfamiliar words, names or places.

6. Use the prayer suggestion to guide you in thanking God for what you have learned and to pray about the applications that have come to mind.

7. You may want to go on to the suggestion under "Now or Later," or you may want to use that idea for your next study.

Suggestions for Members of a Group Study

1. Come to the study prepared. Follow the suggestions for individual study mentioned above. You will find that careful preparation will greatly enrich your time spent in group discussion.

2. Be willing to participate in the discussion. The leader of your group will not be lecturing. Instead, he or she will be encouraging the members of the group to discuss what they have learned. The leader will be asking the questions that are found in this guide.

3. Stick to the topic being discussed. Your answers should be based on the verses which are the focus of the discussion and not on outside authorities such as commentaries or speakers. These studies focus on a particular passage of Scripture. Only rarely should you refer to other portions of the Bible. This allows for everyone to participate in in-depth study on equal ground.

4. Be sensitive to the other members of the group. Listen attentively when they describe what they have learned. You may be surprised by their insights! Each question assumes a variety of answers. Many questions do not have "right" answers, particularly questions that aim at meaning or application. Instead the questions push us to explore the passage more thoroughly.

When possible, link what you say to the comments of others. Also, be affirming whenever you can. This will encourage some of the more hesitant members of the group to participate.

5. Be careful not to dominate the discussion. We are sometimes so eager to express our thoughts that we leave too little opportunity for others to respond. By all means participate! But allow others to also.

6. Expect God to teach you through the passage being discussed and through the other members of the group. Pray that you will have an enjoyable and profitable time together, but also that as a result of the study you will find ways that you can take action individually and/or as a group.

7. Remember that anything said in the group is considered confidential and should not be discussed outside the group unless specific permission is given to do so.

8. If you are the group leader, you will find additional suggestions at the back of the guide.

1

In Search of the King

Matthew 1—2

For our twenty-fifth wedding anniversary we visited friends in London. During our stay there, we planned to take the Eurostar train under the English Channel to Paris. In the months before our departure, our upcoming trip kept popping up in our conversations—at the dinner table, driving in the car or sitting in the backyard.

GROUP DISCUSSION. Describe something you once strongly desired (for example, a car, TV, stereo or special relationship). When you got it, did it fulfill your expectations? Explain why or why not.

PERSONAL REFLECTION. What are you currently waiting for or anticipating? How does it affect your thoughts during the day?

The long-awaited birth of the Messiah is recorded in Matthew 1—2. The nation of Israel waited for centuries for God's anointed king to be born. What a wonderful day that was to be. Jesus' birth, however, was not greeted with royal gladness by the nation and its leaders. Instead there was intrigue and conflict. The political and religious establishment felt threatened by the coming of the Messiah. It was left to foreign leaders to welcome the newborn king. *Read Matthew 1.*

1. Considering the portrayal of Jesus as a heavenly king, why would

Matthew include a lineage at the very beginning of his book?

2. In a dream, Joseph receives a visit from an angel (vv. 16-24). What comfort would the angel's message have brought to Joseph?

What anxieties might it have created?

3. *Read Matthew 2.* In this chapter Matthew portrays Jesus' initial reception by the world. Compare and contrast Jesus the heavenly king with Herod the earthly king.

4. There are many traditions and myths in church history about the Magi that may or may not be true. Drawing only from the information in this passage, what can we discover about them?

5. Describe the details of their search for Jesus.

6. How has knowing Jesus involved you in a search or journey?

7. How are the Magi different from the religious leaders in this passage?

8. Jesus was born during the time of King Herod (v. 1). From your reading of this chapter, what was Herod like?

9. On hearing of Jesus' birth from the searching Magi, Herod also begins a search for the newborn Christ. How does his search compare with that of the Magi?

10. The responses of the Magi and Herod are typical of the ways people respond to Jesus today. What factors might cause people to respond to Jesus in such radically different ways?

11. God is the unseen actor throughout the chapter. In what ways can we detect his behind-the-scenes actions (2:6, 15, 23)?

12. The Magi not only found Jesus but worshiped him and witnessed to the entire city of Jerusalem concerning his birth (2:2-3). In what ways has your search for the Lord resulted in your worshiping him and telling others about him?

Spend time worshiping the King of kings. Then ask God to help you tell others about him.

Now or Later

It is helpful to get a perspective on how Matthew put his book together. An overview of Matthew also draws together seemingly isolated events and teachings into a meaningful whole.

13. Matthew's theme statement is found in the last three verses of the last chapter. *Read 28:18-20.* What is the theme?

14. Matthew wants us to see Jesus as a heavenly king. What attributes of a king do you see portrayed in these three verses?

15. How do you think this concern may have affected Matthew's writing throughout his book?

16. *Skim chapters 1-4.* Matthew has recorded the things Jesus taught and commanded his disciples to teach others. What did Matthew feel a disciple should know about the beginnings of Jesus' ministry?

17. In chapters 5-7 we have a summary of the King's laws. As you skim these laws, what responses do you have?

What does Jesus expect of his disciples?

18. In chapters 8-9 the miracles of Jesus play a dominant part. In what ways are faith and authority a part of this section?

19. In the midst of widening conflict and controversy, Jesus reveals his true identity to the disciples (10:1—16:20). How does he do this in 14:1—16:20?

20. What do you hope to gain from studying Matthew?

2

Preparing for the King

Matthew 3

In ancient times the coming of a king required special preparation. A herald was sent ahead to prepare the road on which the king would be traveling. Holes were filled, rough places made smooth and crooked sections straightened. The same thing happened in recent times when Queen Elizabeth II visited the Bahamas. In preparation for her coming, the roads she would be traveling on were completely resurfaced.

GROUP DISCUSSION. Historically kings were the embodiment of authority. Royal figures today are more often media curiosities. Political figures are more familiar to us. What responses do you have when you read of visits of political authorities to your city? Why?

PERSONAL REFLECTION. Appearing before a king was keenly anticipated, for it provided an opportunity to make a personal request. It also created anxiety—there might be an inquiry into personal conduct. Examine your heart. What requests might you make of God as the ultimate authority? What would you be anxious about?

In Matthew 3 John the Baptist is sent to prepare the way for the coming of the Lord. But his arrival required a very different kind of preparation. *Read Matthew 3.*

1. What are your initial impressions of John?

---

2. For Israel the desert was a place of both punishment and renewal (recall the wilderness wanderings). How does John's ministry convey both concepts (vv. 3-12)?

---

3. The religious leaders considered themselves children of Abraham (v. 9). According to verses 7-10, how were they abusing this privilege?

---

4. What are some ways Christians today abuse their rights as children of God?

---

5. John calls us to produce "fruit in keeping with repentance" (v. 8). Give examples of the kind of fruit you think he has in mind.

---

6. John and Jesus have ministries of baptism (vv. 11-12). How are their baptisms similar and different?

---

7. Why do you think John was hesitant to baptize Jesus (vv. 13-14)?

8. What does Jesus' willingness to be baptized suggest about him (v. 15)?

In what ways was Jesus' baptism different from other baptisms?

9. What significance do you see in the dove and the voice from heaven at Jesus' baptism (vv. 16-17)?

10. The coming of Christ either demands repentance or brings judgment. In what ways do you need to better prepare for his return?

11. Think of people around you who face rough places or valleys. How can you help them smooth out the rough places or fill in the valleys in preparation for Jesus' coming?

Ask God to give you the courage to speak boldly and the wisdom to speak perceptively about the ministry of Jesus Christ to friends and relatives.

Now or Later

John the Baptist communicates clearly that God expects fruit to be produced from a life of godliness. If you are working through this study in a small group, tell one another what fruit you see in each other. Let this be a time of affirmation and care.

If you are studying on your own, gently ask yourself the question, *What fruit do I see in my life?* Make a list of what you discover.

3

The Beginning
of the Kingdom

Matthew 4

"Is it time yet?" "How much longer?" Those are the questions our children asked repeatedly as Christmas approached. It was hard for them (and us) to wait. But when Christmas Day came, it was full of fun and surprises. After weeks of waiting, the wrapping finally came off. We all got to put on or play with our new gifts.

GROUP DISCUSSION. Recall a time when you experienced something new—starting a new job, going to a new school, moving to a new community. Starting something new always brings testing and challenges. How do you respond when you face threatening obstacles or unexpected resistance?

PERSONAL REFLECTION. Challenges and difficulties provide an opportunity to rely in new ways on God and his Word. Consider the challenges you are facing and place each one before the Lord. In your mind's eye turn each one over to him and ask him what to do. Spend some time quietly listening for the wisdom and insight he will give you.

The beginning of Jesus' ministry was like the coming of Christmas. After a long wait, the wraps came off and the world got to see God's greatest gift. In an amazingly short period of time Jesus comes from the desert, calls his disciples together and is soon surrounded by crowds. How did all this happen so fast? *Read Matthew 4.*

1. Look over the entire chapter to discover the locations mentioned. What do they tell us about Jesus' ministry?

2. Prior to beginning his ministry Jesus must face testing and temptation (vv. 1-11). Look specifically at each temptation (vv. 3-4, 5-7, 8-10). What do you think Satan was trying to accomplish?

3. The prerequisite for Jesus' ministry was his ability to resist temptation. What insights into Jesus' character does this encounter with Satan provide?

4. What can you learn about temptation and how to resist it from Jesus' example?

5. Verses 12-17 describe the transition from testing to ministry. What do they tell us about Jesus and his agenda?

6. Jesus moves into Galilee with a message about the kingdom of heaven (v. 17). One of Jesus' first functions as king is calling disciples. From verses 18-22, develop a brief description of what is required for "citizenship" in his kingdom.

7. Citizenship for the disciples meant leaving job and family, and following Jesus wherever he went. How has discipleship affected your life?

8. In verses 23-25 Matthew gives us a summary of Jesus' initial public ministry. Describe the people who came looking for Jesus.

9. Imagine the excitement of the first disciples as they watched Jesus healing and teaching among the crowds. Put yourself in their place and describe how you would feel.

10. In what way would you like to meet or experience Jesus in your own life?

Ask the Lord to allow you to share in the excitement of his message and ministry and to share with others.

Now or Later

Jesus preached the good news. Both his message and his presence were good news. Spend some time each day just sitting in the presence of the Lord. Perhaps you could sit in front of an empty chair and see him there in your mind's eye. Sit until you find yourself settling and quieting down.

4

The Law of the King
(Part 1)

Matthew 5:1—6:18

C. S. Lewis was once criticized for not caring for the Sermon on the Mount. He replied, "As to 'caring for' the Sermon on the Mount, if 'caring for' here means 'liking' or enjoying, I suppose no one 'cares for' it. Who can like being knocked flat on his face by a sledgehammer? I can hardly imagine a more deadly spiritual condition than that of a man who can read that passage with tranquil pleasure."*

Lewis was right. Studying the Sermon on the Mount can be a devastating experience. It exposes the depth of our sin and the shallowness of our commitment. But the pain it inflicts is meant to heal, not destroy, us. In fact, the Sermon on the Mount could be called the Christian's job description. It is the most complete summary we have of Jesus' ethical expectations for his followers. Throughout church history it has been a helpful guide and a convicting challenge.

GROUP DISCUSSION. Have everyone in your group write several guidelines for your group's meetings. The guidelines could encompass content, time, meeting structure, components and more. Once you have shared these, discuss how each set of guidelines expresses the character of the person who wrote it. Consider too how the suggested guidelines would shape the character of the group.

PERSONAL REFLECTION. Godly men and women in the Old Testament considered God's law a wonderful gift (as opposed to a burden or oppressive obligations). In your mind's eye receive the gift of God's law from him wrapped in colorful paper. Spend a few moments being thankful that he loves you enough to tell you what is best for you.

Jesus' teaching about the behavior required of citizens of his kingdom is both comprehensive and intensive. He covers everything from personal relationships to religious responsibilities to daily needs of food, clothing and shelter. The teaching is intensive: it is addressed not only to our outward behavior but to our internal motivations. This study looks at the first half of the Sermon on the Mount and Jesus' teaching on motivation and religious responsibilities. *Read Matthew 5.*

---

1. What responses do you have as you read Jesus' teaching on the law and relationships?

---

2. The Beatitudes describe the qualities Jesus requires of those who live as citizens of his kingdom (vv. 3-12). What would it feel like to be a member of a community of people who shared these qualities?

---

3. Each beatitude comes with specific blessings. In what ways could a community possessing such blessings be described as rich?

---

4. Jesus compares his followers to salt and light (vv. 13-16). What do these metaphors suggest about our role in society?

5. In the rest of chapter 5 Jesus discusses various misconceptions we might have about the Law (Old Testament Scriptures). Why do you think that Jesus stresses that he did not come to abolish the Law (vv. 17-20)?

———————————————————————————————

6. Jesus' teaching on murder and adultery (vv. 21-30) differs from traditional understanding. How would it clarify and cleanse the way the citizens of his kingdom are to live?

———————————————————————————————

7. In verses 31-37 Jesus provides instructions on divorce and oaths (legal relationships) that confront Jewish tradition. How do his changes confront the issue of duplicity?

———————————————————————————————

8. In verses 38-47 Jesus teaches on enemies and evil people. How does Jesus' teaching shape the way his citizens respond to opposition?

———————————————————————————————

9. Verse 48 summarizes the essence of what Jesus has been saying. What responses do you have to Jesus' high standard?

———————————————————————————————

10. *Read Matthew 6:1-18.* Jesus shifts his focus from relationships to "religious obligations." What do we learn about proper and improper motives from Jesus' examples about giving, praying and fasting?

11. Looking back on all you have read in the Sermon on the Mount, how are motives central to Jesus' teaching on both relationships and religious acts?

---

12. How does Jesus' teaching on motives address your experience of the Christian life?

Ask the Lord to work his character into your heart so that his light might shine from your life.

Now or Later

The Ten Commandments could be described as the beatitudes of the Old Testament. They are the introduction and summary of what God required of Israel as his covenant people. Turn to Exodus 20:1-12 and read over the first five commandments. How does each one express the character of God?

How might each one shape your character?

God in the Dock (Grand Rapids, Mich.: Eerdmans, 1970), pp. 181-82.

5

The Law of the King
(Part 2)

Jim Elliot, a missionary killed by the Auca Indians, once wrote: "He is no fool who gives what he cannot keep to gain what he cannot lose." His words echo this portion of the Sermon on the Mount. Jesus asks us to choose between two treasures, two masters, two roads and two destinies. But he clearly explains why following him is the only wise choice.

GROUP DISCUSSION. It is often difficult to put off buying what we want till we can afford it. What internal and external pressures make it difficult to wait? When have you put off buying something you wanted because you knew it would be better to wait awhile? Why?

PERSONAL REFLECTION. Earthly treasures are often more tempting than heavenly ones. We need to work on learning to see the riches of heaven with an inward eye. Picture a great pile of treasure waiting for you to use in "heart-satisfying" ways. Once you have it in view, how would knowing that it is waiting for you affect the way you would live out the rest of the day?

While the first section of the Sermon on the Mount focuses on inward motivations, the last half of it is focused on "upward" motivations. *Read Matthew 6:19-34.*

1. In 6:19-24 Jesus talks about treasures, eyes and masters. What

common themes tie these verses together?

2. Worry is a dominant theme in 6:25-34. How can we escape worrying about such things as food and clothes?

3. What sorts of things do you worry about?

How might Jesus' teaching help you?

4. The Sermon on the Mount tells what we must do to seek first God's kingdom and righteousness (6:33). What does the little word *first* do to our understanding and application of his teaching?

5. *Read Matthew 7.* What is the difference between judging others and being properly discerning (7:1-6)?

6. In what ways have you seen relationships in the church hurt by Christians judging each other?

7. What would it feel like to live in a community that understood the difference between judging and discerning?

8. Jesus' laws for the citizens of his kingdom are extremely demanding. What hope does he provide for help (7: 7-11)?

9. In the final section of the Sermon (7:13-27) Jesus talks about narrow and wide gates, good and bad trees, and wise and foolish builders. How do these metaphors work together to make a common point?

What reason are we given for obeying Jesus' teaching?

10. What distinguishes genuine prophets and followers from false ones (7:15-23)?

11. Putting Jesus' words into practice is the way to build a lasting foundation against the day of judgment (7:24-27). What will practicing Jesus' Sermon require of you?

Pray that God will give you the resources to live by the law of his kingdom.

Now or Later

Self-examination is an important spiritual activity. Examine yourself in a time of leisurely silence and reflection in the following areas: Divided loyalty or divine allegiance? Trust for or worry about daily provision? Careless behavior or cautious conduct? Foolish following or discerning reflection? Empty talk or a consistent walk? Endurance in times of difficulties or surrender to doubt?

What needs to change for you to live as a good citizen of the kingdom?

6

The Powers of the King

Matthew 8:1—9:34

Someone once commented about a U.S. president in the last half of the twentieth century, "I don't know where he is going, but I sure like the way he leads." Leaders must demonstrate authority as they show initiative. But wise leaders know they must not abuse their authority in pursuit of their agenda. People who follow leaders with a sense of loyal allegiance look for someone who demonstrates not only authority but also integrity and compassion.

GROUP DISCUSSION. Consider the leadership of your (a) church, (b) place of employment or (c) city or town. How does the character of the leadership shape the "tone" and "feel" of each?

PERSONAL REFLECTION. Think of someone in your life who has significantly influenced you. How did you come to respect that person?

In the Sermon on the Mount, Jesus impressed the crowd with his authoritative teaching. In chapters 8 and 9 he displays his authority to heal sickness and sin. As he does so, Jesus demonstrates that he is a worthy king in whom we can safely put our trust. *Read Matthew 8:1-22.*

---

1. In chapters 8-9 Jesus' miracles occur in three groups, followed by a response. Describe how Jesus demonstrates his authority in 8:1-22.

2. Lepers were outcasts in Jewish society and were required to shout "unclean" wherever they went. What impresses you about Jesus' encounter with the man in 8:1-4?

3. In your life, how has a relationship with Christ made a difference between feeling included in or excluded from meaningful contact with others?

4. Jesus is pleased with the centurion's response (8:5-13). What makes the centurion a good model of faith?

5. In 8:18-22 we see how Jesus responds to would-be followers. From what Jesus says to them, what is he looking for?

What might Jesus say to you if you walked up to him today and volunteered to be a disciple?

6. *Read Matthew 8:23—9:17.* The disciples' fear of the furious storm seems natural (8:23-27). What sort of faith is Jesus looking for in his disciples?

7. After what had happened to the demon-possessed men, the townspeople pleaded with Jesus to leave their region (8:28-34). Why?

8. What are some reasons today why people don't want Jesus Christ around?

---

9. Jesus' claim to have authority to forgive sins as he heals the paralytic (9:1-8) upset and assaulted the religious system of his day. How do you respond when you find someone competing with your authority or displacing you?

---

10. In 9:9-17 Jesus compares himself to a doctor and a bridegroom, and then discusses garments and wineskins. What is Jesus teaching us about his kingdom and its impact through these illustrations?

---

11. *Read Matthew 9:18-34.* Notice the problems over which Jesus displays power and authority in these verses. How might this picture of Jesus strengthen your faith in the challenges that you face?

Ask the Lord to strengthen your vision of his power in ways that deepen your faith.

Now or Later

Make a list or begin a journal of your prayer requests and the answers you receive. Pay attention to how this record of the Lord's actions in your life provides rich fertilizer for a growing faith.

7

The Messengers of the King

During the late 1800s a wealthy philanthropist decided to give away all his money. He announced he would give five hundred dollars to anyone with a legitimate need. As you might imagine, the response was overwhelming! But more than financial help, people have a need for the spiritual riches of the gospel.

GROUP DISCUSSION. If you were sent out to the local mall to spend the day telling people about Jesus and his message, what sort of experiences do you think you could expect?

PERSONAL REFLECTION. Whether we like it or not, taking risks is an essential part of discipleship. Ask God to show you issues in your heart that keep you from following through.

Jesus sends out the Twelve on their own mission assignment. As he sends them out, he empowers them with the ability to meet needs yet warns them about the dangers that come from helping people. *Read Matthew 9:35—11:1.*

---

1. Jesus has compassion for the crowds (9:35-38) who were "harassed and helpless." How are people today similar to those Jesus cared for?

2. As a result of his compassion for the crowds, Jesus sends out the Twelve (10:1-15). Describe their mission.

What would it feel like to take on this mission?

3. Jesus warns the disciples that their compassionate ministry will not be warmly received (10:16-25). What will they experience?

4. In 10:26-33 Jesus prepares his present and future disciples for opposition. Why shouldn't the disciples be afraid of those who oppose them?

5. Following Christ may strain family relationships and loyalties (10:32-39). Why should we risk such tensions?

What promises are made in 10:40-42?

6. *Read Matthew 11:2-30.* John appears to be experiencing frustration and second thoughts because of his imprisonment. What might (or perhaps has) given you frustrations and second thoughts about Jesus?

7. How would you describe the tone and feel of Jesus' reply to John (11:4-6)?

8. What does 11:7-19 tell us about John and those who heard his message?

9. In 11:20-30 Jesus denounces some people and offers a warm invitation to others. What causes his denunciations?

10. This section ends as it began, with an expression of Jesus care and compassion (11:28-30). In what ways have you found rest in your life by coming to Jesus?

Pray for the gift of rest and peace that come to those who respond to Jesus' invitation.

Now or Later

Although we don't always have to physically leave our families, nor do we always experience their rejection, Jesus Christ must always be first in our hearts. Close your eyes and picture each family member or person to whom you have intimate ties. Give each one to the Lord for his care and protection. Tell the Lord that he is first in your life. As you yield them to the Lord, notice your heart responses.

8

The Leaders
& the King

Matthew 12

There was a small stand of trees not far from my house when I was growing up where we loved to build forts. More than once a new fort went unused or was even torn down because we could not agree on who got to be in charge. Power is not easily shared. With neighborhood children such disagreements may be amusing. But the struggle over power is serious. History is littered with destruction and death from disputes over who gets to be in charge.

GROUP DISCUSSION. Share an experience of leadership in which you encountered resistance. How did you feel, and how did you handle it?

PERSONAL REFLECTION. Passive resistance, biting humor, spreading rumors and outright resistance are just four of the many ways to compete for or resist power. Which is your preferred style?

Like ripples in a pool of water, the ministry of Jesus and his disciples continued to have a widening impact on the Jewish nation. Seeing his power, the Jewish leader began formulating a strategy to discredit him. *Read Matthew 12.*

1. How would you describe the feel of this chapter?

2. Consider the ways that religious leaders attacked Jesus in verses 1-14. What was their strategy?

_____

3. The first attack on Jesus is indirect; the leaders aim at the disciples (vv. 3-8). What is their charge, and how does Jesus answer it?

_____

4. How are similar arguments used today to discredit Christianity?

_____

5. The irony in the second assault of the Pharisees is that while Jesus is healing on the sabbath, the Pharisees are making plans to kill him, (vv. 8-12). How does Jesus' attitude toward people and Scripture differ from that of the Pharisees?

_____

6. How have you been impacted by issues of religious authority?

_____

7. In the first two conflicts Jesus embodies the Old Testament Scripture that Matthew quotes (vv. 15-21). Why is Jesus worthy to be followed?

_____

8. In their third assault the Pharisees charge that Jesus' power over demons is demonic (vv. 25-37). If people believed the Pharisees, how would it affect Jesus' ministry?

9. Why might the request for a sign from the leader be met with such resounding condemnation at this point in the conflict (vv. 38-42)?

10. In verses 43-45 Jesus tells the Pharisees and teachers of the Law a story. What does it reveal about them?

11. Self-reform is futile because of the power of evil. What hope, if any, can there be for the leaders?

12. In our personal lives and in our churches, how can we avoid being like the Pharisees and the teachers of the Law?

What area of change in your life should you consider changing?

Ask God to teach you how to read and understand his Word so that you can live under its authority with integrity.

Now or Later

One of the ways we resist God is by finding excuses for avoiding Scripture reading or prayer. Keep a journal of times you "avoid" being alone with God. If you are in a small group, be prepared to share your findings with your group at a future meeting.

9

The Parables of the King

Matthew 13

One of the quickest ways I know to bring an unruly classroom under control is to tell a story. The noise and bickering end as children are drawn into the adventure or mystery. (I also find that telling a story is a great way to bring back wandering minds during my sermons!)

GROUP DISCUSSION. Share a few of your favorite authors and stories. Be sure to tell just what it is you like about them.

PERSONAL REFLECTION. If you chose to tell the story of your life, what would you describe as the climax? How would God be seen in the plot?

Jesus speaks to a fickle crowd. Some are hungry to hear his message. Others are suspicious and hostile. In this setting Jesus begins to teach in parables. These stories test our spiritual sight and hearing. They also expose the condition of our hearts. *Read Matthew 13.*

1. What initial impressions do you have of the kingdom of heaven?

2. According to the parable of the sower, what responses does Jesus expect as he preaches his message about the kingdom (vv. 1-9, 18-23)?

3. How would this parable be a challenge to his listeners?

How does it challenge you?

4. How would Jesus' parables be the proper remedy for the spiritual people he is speaking to (vv. 11-17)?

5. Jesus has in mind the mixed nature of his crowd as he tells the parable of the wheat and weeds (vv. 24-30, 36-43). What lessons might this parable have for disciples and members of the church?

6. How would the parables of the mustard seed and yeast address the expectation that the kingdom of God was to be brought in by a mighty revolution against the military aggressors of Israel (vv. 31-35)?

7. The gospel of the kingdom continues to be a present power in the world though the ministry of God's Word and Spirit. What are the practical implications of the parables we have looked at so far for mission and evangelism?

8. The parables of the hidden treasure and the pearl teach the supreme value of the kingdom (vv. 44-46). How has the supreme value of the kingdom affected your use of resources?

9. This chapter concludes with a visit to Jesus' hometown. How do the people there compare with those described in verses 13-15?

10. How might familiarity with spiritual truth be an obstacle to spiritual insight?

11. Jesus wants his disciples to understand the parables. How have they enlarged your understanding of the kingdom of heaven?

12. Jesus also wants us to respond to what we have heard and understood. Throughout this chapter, what types of responses does he desire?

Ask the Lord to make you responsive to the mysteries of the kingdom of God.

Now or Later

The nature of spiritual blindness is that those who are blind don't know it. And the nature of sin is that none of us are immune. Begin each day this week by asking God to bring to mind areas of spiritual blindness in your life. At the end of each day note insights that come to mind. If you are in a small group, report what you discover.

10

The Revelation of the King

Matthew 14

Crises are uncomfortable. If we had our choice, we would prefer a smooth life experience without difficulties. But life in this world just doesn't work that way. The good news is that Christians understand from the Scriptures that behind every crisis is the hand of God who is using the crisis to shape our character and further his work in the world.

GROUP DISCUSSION. Consider a difficult time in your life. Describe what happened and how God used it to shape your character.

PERSONAL REFLECTION. What is your first response when you are in difficult circumstances? How does your faith affect the way you handle crises?

The focus shifts from parables about the kingdom to the identity of the King. In order to deepen the disciples' understanding about who he is, Jesus places them in tough situations in which they must act on what they have learned about him. *Read Matthew 14.*

---

1. In verses 1-2 Herod speculates about Jesus' identity. What leads him to believe that Jesus is John the Baptist (vv. 3-12)?

2. Herod, although a king, was a slave of people's opinion. In what ways do the opinions of others shape your behavior in general and your responsiveness to God in particular?

3. John the Baptist and Jesus were linked both by their families and their ministries. What clues might such a connection provide for Jesus' withdrawal to a solitary place (v. 13)?

4. Describe the circumstances, setting and people present during the feeding of the five thousand (vv. 13-21). How is this a test for the disciples in their knowledge of Jesus and his mission?

5. Herod and Jesus, the two kings, both serve banquets. What does each king's banquet reveal about his character and authority?

6. Imagine you are with the anxious disciples in the boat (vv. 22-26). Describe what you would see, hear and feel.

7. Peter's experience is a vivid picture of faith and doubt (vv. 28-31). When are you most tempted to take your eyes off the Lord and to sink in doubt?

8. In verse 33 the disciples worship Jesus and declare, "Truly you are the Son of God." What in this incident leads you to worship Jesus?

_____

9. How can the disciples' experience help you to trust Jesus the next time you are tempted to doubt?

_____

10. Through these puzzling experiences with Jesus the disciples come to confess that he is the Son of God. What experiences have helped you understand more about the Lord?

_____

11. What factors contributed to the difference in the recognition of the crowds (vv. 34-36) from the recognition of the disciples (v. 33)?

_____

12. What experiences and insights have led you into a deeper worship experience of Jesus?

Spend a few minutes worshiping Jesus, the Son of God.

Now or Later

According to the glimpse into heaven in Revelation 4—5, the chief activity of heaven is the worship of God. Each day this week choose one thing that can be an inspiration to worship God. Perhaps one day it might be a sunset; next it might be the pleasure of a good meal.

11

Understanding the King

Matthew 15:1—16:20

Along with stories, questions were one of the essential tools of both Jesus and his disciples. Teachers use questions to get students to look deeper. On the other hand, students use questions to gain information and to explore what they don't understand.

GROUP DISCUSSION. Ask members of your group two or three questions that will help you understand something new about their background and character.

PERSONAL REFLECTION. If God were to ask several questions about your actions and thoughts this past week, what might he ask?

Step by step the disciples come to a new understanding of Jesus. What they thought they knew becomes a new and deeper knowledge. Peter, speaking for the disciples, confesses that Jesus is the Christ, the Son of God. With Peter's confession we come to the climax of the first half of Matthew. *Read Matthew 15.*

---

1. In verses 1-2 top religious leaders from Jerusalem oppose Jesus by attacking the disciples. What extensive steps does Jesus take to confront their accusation (vv. 3-20)?

2. How would you describe the tone of Jesus' response?

3. What religious practices in your life or your church might be in danger of becoming outward, empty forms?

How can you avoid this tendency?

4. Jesus is not only hard on the Pharisees, he is hard on the Canaanite woman who seeks his help. How would you explain the strange interaction between Jesus, the woman and the disciples (vv. 21-28)?

5. How was this woman the antithesis of the Pharisees in the preceding section?

6. *Read Matthew 16:1-20.* After Jesus heals the sick and feeds the four thousand, the religious leaders ask him for a sign from heaven (16:1). Why do you think Jesus refuses them (16:2-4)?

7. In 16:5-12 the disciples misunderstand Jesus' allusion to yeast. How is their misunderstanding related to a lack of faith?

8. There is a notable leap in spiritual insight in 16:13-20 as the disciples, who couldn't even grasp a simple figure of speech, suddenly through Peter declare that Jesus is the Christ, the Son of God (16:13-17). How do you account for the sudden change?

9. What is the role of grace in spiritual insight?

How might that affect the way you study the Bible and listen to sermons?

10. How would you describe the tone of Jesus' response to Peter?

11. How will Peter's confession of Jesus as the Christ, the Son of God, unlock the entrance to the kingdom of heaven for others (16:18-20)?

12. Jesus' question to Peter is a question that the entire human race will have to respond to at some point. Who do you say Jesus is and why?

Ask Jesus to use you to be a means of spiritual insight for others.

Now or Later

Review Matthew 1:1—16:20. Summarize what you have learned about Jesus' law, power, character and mission. Then summarize what you've learned about the challenges of being a disciple of Jesus.

12

The Work of the King

Matthew 16:21—17:27

One of the rules of good leadership is "no surprises." Surprises can be upsetting. However, the no-surprise mentality can also become a formula for monotony and drudgery. I believe there is wisdom in the no-surprise mentality, but I like variety and want to adjust it a bit. Instead I say, "Good leadership seeks to eliminate unplanned surprises."

GROUP DISCUSSION. There is a significant difference between a pleasant surprise and an unpleasant surprise. Share one of each that you can recall.

PERSONAL REFLECTION. The unfolding experience of Christian maturity includes surprises from both pain we could never have guessed and joys that we couldn't have anticipated. In what ways has believing in Christ surprised you?

Now that the disciples have been with Jesus for a while, Jesus must prepare them for the true nature of his kingdom. Initially the disciples are surprised as Jesus reveals the shocking cost of his mission and his requirements for discipleship. *Read Matthew 16:21—17:13.*

1. What were some of the surprises the disciples received?

2. Peter and Jesus seem to be at cross-purposes as Jesus' statements do not fit the Jewish expectation of a conquering Messiah who defeats the enemies of Israel. In what specific ways are they different (16:21-23)?

3. Jesus' response to Peter is extremely intense. Why do you think Jesus addressed Peter as Satan?

4. Jesus reveals the ultimate cost of following him (16:24-28), a cost that Peter indeed paid at the end of his life as he was killed in Rome. Why didn't Jesus tell Peter and the disciples about the issue of cost when he first called them?

5. How does the cost of discipleship affect the way you think about the leadership of Jesus?

How does the cost of discipleship affect the way you think about the Christian faith?

6. As he reveals the cost of discipleship, he also speaks of the benefits. How might the transfiguration be a partial fulfillment of Jesus' promise of the impending rewards of the kingdom (16:28—17:9)?

7. What would the disciples learn about Jesus by his transformed appearance, his conversation with Moses and Elijah, and the voice from heaven (17:1-8)?

8. How might the experience of the transfiguration help them cope with their confusion around Jesus' impending death?

9. Having just seen Elijah on the mountain, the disciples are puzzled about the expected future ministry (v. 10) that Malachi writes about in the Old Testament. In what sense was Elijah's ministry fulfilled by John the Baptist (17:11-13)?

10. How was the ministry both a preparation for and a foreshadowing of Jesus' ministry?

11. The unfolding frustration of the disciples continues. *Read Matthew 17:14-27.* Describe your impression of Jesus as he confronts the spiritual powerlessness of his disciples.

12. As a result of their powerlessness the disciples learn more about the nature of faith. What message would they get from Jesus' teaching?

13. Following Jesus is confusing since we don't always understand life from a heavenly perspective. How can this passage help reorient your thinking?

Pray that God will give you the courage to follow in the face of confusion and disorientation.

Now or Later

In the first half of Matthew we were introduced to Jesus and his kingdom. In the last half we will see that Jesus' work went far beyond teaching and healing. At great cost to himself he confronts the powers of darkness and through suffering becomes a mighty victor and deliverer. The questions below provide an overview to the rest of the book.

14. Briefly look over 16:21—17:27. How are the suffering and glory of Jesus' mission displayed in this section?

15. Chapters 18-20 are similar in many ways to the Sermon on the Mount. Read through them quickly, looking for ways the disciples can become great in the kingdom.

16. Describe the ways that Jesus demonstrates his kingly authority as he occupies the temple and the capital city of Israel in chapters 21 and 22.

17. Jesus continues to display kingly authority in chapter 23. What do you discover about the reasons Jesus judges the religious leaders?

18. Jesus wants his disciples to anticipate the future and final coming of his kingdom. How does he create a sense of expectation in chapters 24 and 25?

19. The final events of Jesus' earthly life come to a climax in chapters 26 and 27. As you look over those events, what impressions do you have?

20. Ultimate victory! In chapter 28 Jesus triumphs over suffering, conflict and death. Put yourself in the disciples' place. What might you be feeling?

13

The Greatest in the Kingdom

Matthew 18

Tell a group of children to line up and as they rush to get in line you will hear shouts of "me first!" Adults are more subtle, but the competition to be first continues throughout life. Every culture and society have levels of honor and higher status, and many people work hard to rank high.

GROUP DISCUSSION. In what ways are people of high social standing treated differently from others? What are the standards that our culture uses to determine who is first?

PERSONAL REFLECTION. How do you deal with pressures to pursue a higher social standing (consider your neighborhood, workplace and church)? How does God fit into your aspirations and desires?

The kingdom of God has its own set of standards, and the disciples want to know how to use those standards to be greatest in the kingdom of God. Jesus takes their question seriously but provides another way to think about ranking and social status. *Read Matthew 18.*

---

1. The disciples want to know who is the greatest in the kingdom of heaven (v. 1). How does Jesus' appeal to little children answer their question (vv. 2-5)?

2. Since children have little status in the eyes of adults, how would assuming the status of a child affect you in your circle of friends or coworkers?

3. In the following verses the "little ones" are those who humble themselves ("become like little children") and believe in Jesus. How would you characterize Jesus' attitude toward those who cause the little ones who believe in him to sin (vv. 6-7)?

4. Jesus graphically illustrates the importance of dealing with sin in our own lives (vv. 8-9). What difference might his teaching make in the way we consider our personal conduct and ethical decisions?

5. Describe the character of God displayed by Jesus' concern for lost sheep (vv. 10-14).

6. Greatness in the kingdom is dependent on living a life of forgiveness and mercy. What guidelines does Jesus give for dealing with those who sin against us (vv. 15-20)?

What is difficult about actually practicing the process that Jesus outlines?

7. Forgiving someone once does not always guarantee he or she will not offend us again. How can the parable of the unmerciful servant help us to keep on forgiving (vv. 21-35)?

8. Look back over chapter 18 and summarize the ways Jesus demonstrates the greatness and value of those who believe in him.

9. How does this passage challenge the world's concept of greatness?

10. How should the value Jesus places on his "little ones" affect the way we view ourselves and other believers?

Ask God to help you find contentment alone in his sight and fatherly care.

Now or Later

Make a list of people who have hurt you over the course of your life. Each day this week pray through the list and step by step forgive them. Consider whether you need to speak with them about the way they have affected you.

Make a list of people you have hurt. Pray through the list during the week. Consider whether there are some people you need to approach about forgiving you.

14

Life in the Kingdom

Matthew 19—20

What is really important to you? What makes you feel important? Money? Success? Recognition? Dig a little deeper and you will find a desire to be "first"—to have life on your own terms. The kingdom of God has been called the "Upside Down Kingdom" because it turns our desires on their heads. It seems that our instinctive response of placing ourselves first means that we get everything upside down. Jesus' gift to us is to reorient us.

GROUP DISCUSSION. In *The Seven Habits of Highly Effective People* Stephen Covey offers an exercise to help us look at the values we live by: Write out a statement summarizing what you want others to say about you when you die. Do that now as a first try or rough draft. (If you really get into this, you could spend weeks working on it.) What do you want people to say about you? Allow each member of the group to share his or her statement.

PERSONAL REFLECTION. What does success mean to you?

Jesus continues to confuse his disciples. His standards seem impossibly high, and his expectation of allegiance from his disciples is totally consuming. How are they ever going to figure out what it means to be a citizen of the kingdom? *Read Matthew 19.*

1. Describe Jesus' teaching on marriage and divorce (vv. 1-12).

Why do you think the disciples were so shocked by what he was saying?

_____

2. Jesus' teachings on divorce and remarriage contrast with those of our culture. What is his point?

_____

3. When children are brought to Jesus in verses 13-15, the disciples demonstrate that they have not yet learned what Jesus has been teaching them about greatness in the kingdom of heaven. Why do you think this is so hard to understand?

_____

4. Wealth was considered a sign of God's favor and a reward for righteous living. Jesus challenges this concept (vv. 16-30). By observing this religious young man struggle between choosing wealth or eternal life, what do we learn about the kingdom?

_____

5. Jesus too offers a form of wealth to his followers. How would you describe it (vv. 27-30)?

How is it obtained?

---

6. There is tension between kingdom wealth and worldly wealth. How might that tension express itself in your life?

---

7. *Read Matthew 20.* Picture yourself in each of the groups of workers described. How would you feel in these differing situations?

---

8. What does the parable of the workers teach us about grace, work and compensation in the kingdom of God (20:1-16)?

---

9. What parts of Jesus' teaching can be applied to the church or other forms of Christian service?

---

10. How does Jesus' statement about his impending death model the values of the kingdom that he has been teaching (vv. 17-19)?

11. Even the mother of James and John gets in on the disciples' struggle to obtain of place of honor and status in Jesus' kingdom (vv. 20-23). Surprisingly Jesus does not condemn the desire. How does he transform it (vv. 24-28)?

Why is it difficult for us to follow Jesus' teaching and example?

12. How does Jesus' interaction with the two blind men illustrate the values he has just taught?

Pray that God would give you the desire and the strength to pursue greatness according to the way of Jesus.

Now or Later

Look back over Jesus' teaching on status, wealth and the conduct expected in his kingdom from chapters 18-20. What do they demonstrate about his character?

Read over chapters 18-20, and make a list of guidelines for discipleship.

15

The King Occupies His Capital

Occasionally someone will say, "I never discuss religion or politics." And in the same vein it is said, "religion and politics don't mix." Such attitudes and postures spring from the heated and emotional "discussions" that religion and politics can produce.

GROUP DISCUSSION. Share views about some current political issue and how your faith is involved in the position you hold. (As you do, notice how much light and heat is generated.)

PERSONAL REFLECTION. How does it affect your prayer life to know that God is working in, through and beyond public officials to display his power and compassion?

In Matthew 21 Jesus' popularity reaches its zenith. In the midst of public acclamation he "occupies" Jerusalem, the capital of the Jewish nation and enters into the temple, which could be described as the heart of the Jewish nation. His clash with the religious leaders reveals what happens when faith and entrenched authority clash. *Read Matthew 21:1-27.*

---

1. As Jesus enters Jerusalem during Passover; excitement is building and emotions are intense. Identify words or phrases that communicate something of the electrifying atmosphere.

2. How do you think the disciples felt as they witnessed the excitement of the crowds and saw Jesus riding on a donkey, fulfilling a prophecy about the Messiah?

3. What different perceptions does the crowd have of Jesus (vv. 9-11)?

4. Are there times when you have been swept up in the public celebration of Jesus? How do these affect you?

5. Jesus the Messiah, having received the praise of the people, enters the temple, looks around and then clears it out (vv. 12-13). Why might this action in the temple be seen as the catalytic event that led to his crucifixion?

6. How might Jesus' interaction with the blind and lame, children and religious leaders *in the temple* be seen as a snapshot (even climax) of Jesus' entire ministry (vv. 14-17)?

7. Read verses 18-19. Jesus' cursing of the fig tree for not having fruit was symbolic of the preceding events. Look back at his entrance into the temple (vv. 12-14). What fruit was Jesus looking for?

---

8. When Jesus reenters the temple on the next day, he is met by angry leaders who demand an explanation for his actions (vv. 23-27). Why is authority the central issue in their confrontation?

---

9. The religious leaders were offended and angry. In order to gain a glimpse of the underlying dynamics of this conflict in the temple, consider how you respond when your authority is questioned in front of friends, coworkers or employees.

---

10. How has the authority of Jesus Christ interrupted, challenged or inconvenienced you?

Ask God to teach you how to submit to the authority of Jesus.

Now or Later

This is a guided meditation. Imagine your heart as a temple into which Jesus walks, looking for the fruit of prayer. As he looks around, what does he see and then what does he say to you? Spend time with this image and use it as a means of conversational prayer with God. Ask him what he would like you to do to be more fruitful. Ask him where you can find fertilizer. Ask him where weeds are that could be pulled out.

16

The King Silences the Opposition

Matthew 21:28—22:46

Confrontation is never easy. Yet there are times when the situation demands it. The religious leaders refused to acknowledge Jesus as God's Messiah. Jesus seeks to expose their hardness of heart and bring them to repentance. They respond not in repentance but by plotting a trap for him.

GROUP DISCUSSION. Role play a conflict between two leaders of your church. One leader wants to change the time of the service from 11:00 a.m. to 10:30 a.m. The other wants no change. Have members of the group help solve the disagreement with a variety of strategies from head-to-head conflict to quiet discussion. How is the emotional tone of the room affected by the conflict?

PERSONAL REFLECTION. The authority of Jesus Christ requires his followers to be subject to him. Spend a few moments laying all your plans for the week at the feet of the Lord. After you have done this, note how it affects your inner disposition.

The conflict between Jesus and the religious leaders takes place as Jesus poses questions and tells parables. *Read Matthew 21:28—22:46.*

---

1. As you look over this section of parables and stories, what common themes can you find?

2. What does the parable of the two sons reveal about the chief priests and elders (21:28-32)?

_____

3. Which son do you most identify with, the one who was passively resistant or the one who was aggressively resistant?

_____

4. The parable of the tenants makes the leaders murderously angry. Why do you think Jesus told it?

_____

5. In the parable of the wedding banquet Jesus illustrates his point that many are invited but few are chosen (22:1-14). What do you think he wanted the religious leaders to understand?

_____

6. After Jesus cleaned out the temple, the religious leaders challenged him with the question "By what authority are you doing these things?" (21:23). How would each of the preceding parables answer this question?

_____

7. In Matthew 22:15-22 the religious leaders discover that direct confrontation with Jesus is not to their advantage, so they seek to trap him with a controversial question. How does Jesus avoid their trap?

8. The Pharisees were unable to trap Jesus over the issue of taxes, so now the Sadducees come forward with a controversial topic of the day: resurrection (22:23-33). How does Jesus handle the situation?

---

9. The next attempt to discredit Jesus revolves around the law. How does his response confront his questioners (22:33-40)?

---

10. Finally, Jesus poses a dilemma to the Pharisees that silences them (22:41-45): "How can the Christ be both the son of David and his Lord?" Why does this question stop them in their tracks?

---

11. Throughout this section Jesus has been involved in verbal battles. How have they confirmed or changed your perception of Jesus?

---

12. Jesus' power to resist his enemies is the same power that he uses to care for his people. What benefits to your relationship with him might come out of this passage?

Thank God for his determination to deliver his people from dominating authorities.

Now or Later

Write a brief story (perhaps a page long) that captures the way the Lord has been working in your life in either conviction or affirmation.

17

The King Condemns
the Rebels

Matthew 23

Influence is a powerful force. Those who influence others are able to change minds and redirect actions. The religious leaders in Israel possessed the power of influence. Once they decided to oppose Jesus, they did their best to lead others to do the same.

GROUP DISCUSSION. Make a list of people who have influenced you. Consider parents, pastors, teachers, political leaders and authors. Note how they have contributed to your character and actions. Consider not only positive influences but negative influences as well and what you have done to overcome their negative impact on your life. Then discuss your lists with one another.

PERSONAL REFLECTION. The Lord guides us not only in the way we should go (Psalm 32:8) but also away from where we should not go. Make a list of things you need to do this week and submit them to the Lord. Ask him for guidance on what your attitudes and actions should be.

The leaders of Israel should have been the first to enter the kingdom of God because of their knowledge of Scripture and their standing in the Jewish community. Because they refused, Jesus calls them to judgment. *Read Matthew 23.*

1. Jesus does not think much of the teachers of the Law and the Pharisees. How would you describe Jesus' words to them and about them?

2. Why do you think Jesus condemns the religious leaders before the whole community in Jerusalem?

3. What attitude does Jesus teach the people to have toward the religious leaders, and why (vv. 1-4)?

4. How are the motives of the disciples (vv. 8-12) to be different from the religious leaders' (vv. 5-7)?

5. Jesus instructs his disciples to avoid being called Rabbi, teacher or father. Why?

6. How can Jesus' instructions to the disciples encourage you to have an attitude of humility?

7. Jesus pronounces seven woes (judgments) against the teachers of the Law and the Pharisees (vv. 13-32). Summarize the point of each one.

8. Jesus condemns the religious leaders for confusing inward and outward righteousness (vv. 25-28). In what ways are we inclined to do that today?

9. The entire generation Jesus is speaking to is held accountable for the "righteous blood shed in all previous generations" (vv. 33-36). Why do you think they received such a terrible sentence?

10. What responses do you have as you observe Jesus as a judge?

11. In the midst of this overwhelming condemnation, how is the tender compassion of Jesus evident (vv. 37-39)?

12. What warnings and hope does this chapter offer us today as we seek to live out our faith?

Ask God to give you a spirit of humility so that no matter who is teaching, you will respond to the Lord as Father, Teacher and Master.

Now or Later

Make a list of all the religious activities that you do, such as attending church, reading the Bible, being in a small group, serving on a committee or doing evangelism. Consider which you are most inclined to do for the approval of others. Which are easier for you to do just because it pleases the Lord?

18

The Return of the King

We want to be safe and secure. Yet many things threaten our security—losing our job, our income, our health, our loved ones. Our ability to handle these threats will depend on the source of our security.

GROUP DISCUSSION. All of us face times that unsettle us. Recall a time that was particularly difficult and share how you got through it.

PERSONAL REFLECTION. The author of Proverbs wrote that the name of the Lord is a strong tower, and the righteous run into it and are safe. As you think about the challenges you face, envision the Lord surrounding you with his strong, powerful presence. Spend a few moments in the safety of his presence before continuing with this study.

Matthew 24 focuses on the destruction of Jerusalem and the return of Christ. The underlying issue that ties together the temple and the return of Christ is where we find the source of our security. *Read Matthew 24.*

---

1. Both the temple's size and its symbolism gave the Israelites a sense of security. When Jesus tells the disciples the temple will be destroyed (vv. 1-2), how do you think they feel?

2. Following Jesus' statement about the temple's destruction, the disciples ask two questions (vv. 1-3). Read through chapter 24 looking for ways that Jesus answers these questions.

3. Throughout history, people have set dates for Christ's return that have been mistaken. What events might deceive the disciples into thinking the end is at hand (vv. 4-8)?

4. Before the end comes, what dangers will believers face, and how are we to handle them (vv. 9-14)?

5. In 167 B.C. Antiochus Epiphanes attacked Jerusalem and set up a pagan altar in the temple—an event that anticipates "the abomination that causes desolation" spoken of by Jesus (v. 15). What occurs in the aftermath of this abomination (vv. 15-22)?

6. In A.D. 70 the Roman general Titus captured Jerusalem and destroyed the temple. Do you think verses 15-22 refer to this event or to events immediately preceding the return of Christ—or both? Explain.

7. Few of us have ever faced deadly peril for our faith. What pressures do you face for your faith in Christ?

---

8. How will we be able to distinguish false Christs from the true Christ (vv. 23-31)?

---

9. The time of Christ's coming is discussed in verses 32-41. What can be known about the timing?

What can't be known?

---

10. How do the parables of the thief and the wise or wicked servant (vv. 42-51) emphasize the importance of living in the light of Christ's return?

---

11. What has this chapter taught you about perseverance and watchfulness?

Give thanks for the confidence and strength that come from Christ's presence by his Word and Spirit, and for the assurance of his return.

Now or Later

Reflect further on what the assurance of Christ's return means for your life, including your choices, goals, priorities and relationships.

19

Preparation for the King's Return

Matthew 25

When I was in seminary, I was a live-in housesitter for a family that traveled frequently. One of my responsibilities during their trips was to keep the plants watered. The first time they traveled I was rather casual, watering only sporadically, if at all. A couple of days before their return date I noticed that the plants weren't doing well: the leaves were yellowish and wilted. Frantically I watered them several times a day and prayed! Thankfully they revived. But I learned my lesson. On all their subsequent trips, I was more careful.

GROUP DISCUSSION. Describe a time, perhaps in school or at work, in which a deadline affected the way you acted.

PERSONAL REFLECTION. The spiritual presence of Christ is not the same as his physical presence. What spiritual benefits come from his physical absence?

Jesus is preparing his disciples for his impending departure. He wants the disciples to know that he holds them accountable for how they conduct themselves in his absence. *Read Matthew 25.*

1. What different dimensions of anticipation do each of the three parables (1:1-13, 14-30, 31-46) emphasize?

2. That only five of the virgins are admitted to the chamber (vv. 1-13) seems harsh. What might be the reasons for such a "hard" parable?

3. What was wrong with the attitude of those who were excluded?

What was right with the attitude of those who were included?

4. Oil for the lamps is a metaphor for being prepared. What do you think is the "oil" you need in order to be prepared for Christ's return?

5. A talent was a vast sum of money. How would you describe the character of the master in the parable of the talents (vv. 14-30)?

6. What was the standard that the master used to judge the servants' behavior?

7. What was defective about the logic that the third servant used to justify his behavior (vv. 24-25)?

8. From this parable, what role do risk and initiative play in being a faithful disciple in the time of the master's extended absence?

9. Early in Jesus' ministry he had compassion on the people "because they were like sheep without a shepherd." In the parable of the sheep and the goats (vv. 31-46) what new insight do we gain about Jesus as a shepherd?

_____

10. In this parable, the images shift from personal master and bridegroom to the ruler of the nations. Identify the King, the sheep, the goats and the "brothers" of the King (vv. 31-46).

_____

11. What criteria does the King use to separate the sheep from the goats?

_____

12. There is an underlying theme of inclusion and exclusion running through these three parables. What is Jesus' point?

_____

13. How does Jesus' teaching broaden your understanding of "hope"?

_____

Ask the Lord to teach you to live with a sense of eternal anticipation.

Now or Later

Anticipation is a strong force for nurturing spiritual growth. Set your expectation for Christ's return to "fast forward." Each morning, determine to live with the expectation that you will see Christ.

20

The Betrayal of the King

On the drizzly day of October 16, 1555, Hugh Latimer and Nicholas Ridley, two influential English Reformers, were tied to the stake as bundles of sticks were piled at their feet. The crowd strained to hear what the two men were saying. Would they recant? As the executioner pushed a torch into the wood, Latimer said, "Be of good comfort, Master Ridley, and play the man; we shall this day light such a candle, by God's grace, in England, as I trust shall never be put out."

GROUP DISCUSSION. Denial of cherished beliefs is a challenge that each generation of believers has to face in some way. Daniel's three friends faced the furnace rather then worship the idol. Do a role play in which three of your members take the role of Daniel's friends. In this scenario, two friends are determined to remain faithful while one is willing to give in. Have the two faithful friends seek to encourage the wavering one to remain faithful. After you have done this exercise, discuss your responses as a group.

PERSONAL REFLECTION. Ponder what influences make you vulnerable to wavering in your faith. As you discover a point of weakness, give each one over to the Lord and ask him what you should do about it.

In Matthew 26 we move into the climax of the book. Both Jesus and his disciples face a time of severe testing. *Read Matthew 26.*

1. This is a lot of Scripture to cover in one lesson, so we will take it by large sections. How do verses 1-16 set the stage for Jesus' betrayal and death?

2. In verses 17-35 Jesus celebrates the Passover with his disciples. How would you describe the atmosphere?

3. From your reading of this passage, consider why partaking of the Lord's supper has become one of the central acts of Christian worship.

4. In light of Matthew's account, what benefits and challenges does the Lord's Supper bring to you as you receive it?

5. The events of denial, desertion and betrayal foretold in verses 1-35 unfold in verses 36-75.

How would you describe Jesus during his dark time in Gethsemane (vv. 36-45)?

6. Jesus exhorts the disciples to "watch and pray so that you will not fall into temptation" (v. 41). What is the relationship between faith, prayer and fear in their upcoming test?

7. Jesus' betrayal comes at the hand of one of his own disciples (vv. 47-50). As you look at the role of Judas in this chapter, why do you think the religious leaders used him?

8. Recent dramatic portrayals of the crucifixion story cast Judas as a disappointed but noble character who loved Jesus but just misunderstood him. Based on Matthew's account, how would you respond to that characterization?

9. Twice during his arrest and once during his interrogation, Jesus states that the Scriptures are being fulfilled (vv. 54, 56, 64). What impact might this have for the various groups surrounding him (that is, the disciples, the crowd, the religious leaders)?

10. Imagine you are in the courtroom where Jesus is being interrogated. Why do you think he remained silent during the first part of his trial (vv. 57-63)?

11. Answering the high priest's question (v. 63), Jesus declares that he is the Christ (alluding to Psalm 110:1 and Daniel 7:14). Describe the immediate—and ultimate—impact of Jesus' words on those present (vv. 65-68).

---

12. Peter's attempt to be courageous turns to cowardice (vv. 69-75). What role do fear and faith occupy in his denial of the Lord?

---

13. Both Jesus and the disciples faced temptation in this chapter. How can Jesus' example and the disciples' failures help us to withstand temptation and testing?

Ask God to give you the courage to believe when you are afraid of difficult circumstances.

Now or Later

Make a list of challenges and temptations that you have faced in the past. Don't show this to anyone. For each "failure" ask God to extend his grace to you afresh. For each "victory" thank God for his strengthing and empowering work inside you that made your victory possible.

21

The Crucifixion of the King

Often our first response to pain is to run from it and deny what we feel, believing life to be easy, smooth and comfortable. In his book *The Road Less Traveled* Scott Peck opened up new levels of personal growth for many by challenging his readers to admit that "life is difficult." Peck goes on to say that most emotional disorders come from the illegitimate avoidance of suffering. Because Jesus taught "Blessed are those who mourn, for they shall be comforted," Christians can say that facing grief and feeling it is the best way through it.

GROUP DISCUSSION. In what specific ways might helping a person mourn in the midst of pain be a better approach than telling someone to "cheer up" or to "keep a stiff upper lip"?

How have you been encouraged or discouraged by others in times of personal grief and loss?

PERSONAL REFLECTION. Somewhere in our hearts there is pain from loss and grief that we have yet to fully face. Ask God to give you courage to face those places of pain so he can comfort you. Rest for a while in his comforting presence.

Matthew 27 records the judgment and execution of Jesus. As Pilate and the religious leaders condemn, mock and crucify God's Son, God himself seems strangely absent. Yet to those who have eyes to see, his presence and power are unmistakable. *Read Matthew 27:1-26.*

1. The chapter begins with the decision by the religious leaders to kill Jesus (v. 1). What do they have to do in order to execute their sentence?

2. Jesus is passive through this entire chapter, yet he is the center of activity. Read through the chapter looking for all the different ways that people respond to him.

3. After the religious leaders hand Jesus over to Pilate, Judas feels remorse (vv. 1-5). How is remorse different from repentance?

4. As Jesus stands before Pilate in verses 11-26, Pilate appears reticent to pronounce a judgment. What crime is Jesus to be executed for?

5. Jesus is caught in the power of both the Jewish religious establishment and the Roman legal system. Why might he have answered one question (v. 11) but refused to defend himself even when Pilate wanted him to?

6. The lordship of Christ means that he's always in charge. In what ways can we deceive ourselves, like Pilate, into thinking Christ serves our purposes instead of submitting to him and his purposes for us?

---

7. *Read Matthew 27:27-66.* As Jesus is beaten and hangs on the cross, he is repeatedly mocked and insulted (vv. 27-44). Why do they mock Jesus?

---

8. As death begins to engulf him, Jesus cries out to God (vv. 45-46). What do his cry and the overshadowing darkness reveal about his relationship to the Father during this torment?

---

9. As the centurion witnesses the strange events surrounding Jesus' death, he exclaims, "Surely he was the Son of God!" (v. 54). What clues do the unusual events referred to in verses 45-56 provide for understanding this chapter?

---

10. Observe the role Jesus' followers play during the events of his crucifixion and burial (vv. 55-61). How do you think they felt?

11. Look over the entire chapter again. How is the character of each person revealed as they respond to Jesus in captivity and death?

---

12. Observe the final measures the chief priests and Pharisees take to insure that their victory over Jesus is complete (vv. 62-66). How does the guarding of the tomb bring together the power of Rome with the power of the Jews?

---

13. This chapter is filled with irony. Satan's "triumph" is actually his defeat. Christ's "defeat" is actually his triumph. How should this challenge our views about the way God works in our lives?

Ask God to give you faith to face the pain of life that comes from living in a world that killed its Savior.

Now or Later

Keep a journal (or perhaps just make a list) each day this week noting your responses to experiences or people that challenge you. As you look over your responses, ask yourself what they show about your faith in God and the quality of your character.

22

The Victory of the King

Matthew 28

The announcement by Franklin Roosevelt that the United States was about to enter World War II meant that life in America would be altered drastically. Likewise, the news of victory at the end of the war meant that life was about to change again. The announcement of the resurrection of Christ from death was an event of even more life-changing proportions.

GROUP DISCUSSION. Sometimes the impact of life-changing events— births of children, moving to a new place, deaths of loved ones— takes time to sink in. What was the most life-changing news that you ever received, and how did it affect you?

PERSONAL REFLECTION. The resurrection of Christ means that he can be with his followers all the time. Spend some time enjoying the presence of Christ and rest in his presence now. In a journal or on a piece of paper write about the difference his presence makes in how you live today.

Matthew 28 focuses on messengers of Jesus' resurrection—the angel tells the women, the women tell the disciples, the disciples tell the nations and the guards tell the religious leaders. *Read Matthew 28.*

1. How do each of those who are involved in the Easter events respond to the empty tomb and the appearances of Jesus?

2. Consider the mission of the women (vv. 1-9). How does it undergo a radical change from their initial approach to the tomb?

3. Neither the women nor the guards were expecting the resurrection or the appearance of angels. What might be a reason for their vastly different responses?

4. The angel is the first messenger of the resurrection (vv. 2-7). How do his message and actions speak to the women's concerns and confusion?

5. At the beginning of Jesus' ministry, John the Baptist prepared the way. Now the angel prepares the way. In what ways is a witness helpful in preparing for a divine encounter?

6. How have you seen the principle of a witness who helps to prepare for an encounter with the Lord active in your own faith and life?

---

7. What does the Jewish leaders' response to the soldiers' report reveal about the leaders' supposed concerns that Jesus might be a false prophet or deceiver (vv. 11-15)?

---

8. The leaders circulated a rumor that the disciples stole the body in order to keep people from believing in Jesus. Why doesn't it make sense to say that the disciples stole Jesus' body?

What keeps people today from believing that Jesus is the resurrected Lord?

---

9. The disciples go to Galilee where they meet with Jesus. How is the experience of the three disciples at the Mount of Transfiguration (Matthew 16:28—17:9) confirmed and expanded on the Mount of Resurrection?

10. Jesus gave to the disciples what we now call the Great Commission. Describe the commission he gives to them and us (vv. 16-20).

---

11. How would this commission sound to the Jewish disciples?

How does it sound to you?

---

12. How would the entire book of Matthew be a helpful tool in fulfilling Jesus' command to make disciples by teaching all that he commanded?

---

13. As you conclude this study of Matthew, how can you be more involved in making disciples and fulfilling the Great Commission?

Ask God to help you take part in being faithful to his commission to his people.

Now or Later

The book of Matthew was the first discipling manual of the early church. Skim through the book of Matthew several times this week looking for as many elements and principles of discipleship as you can find. Write down what you discover that would help you be a better disciple and disciplemaker.

Leader's Notes

MY GRACE IS SUFFICIENT FOR YOU. (2 COR 12:9)

Leading a Bible discussion can be an enjoyable and rewarding experience. But it can also be *scary*—especially if you've never done it before. If this is your feeling, you're in good company. When God asked Moses to lead the Israelites out of Egypt, he replied, "O Lord, please send someone else to do it"! (Ex 4:13). It was the same with Solomon, Jeremiah and Timothy, but God helped these people in spite of their weaknesses, and he will help you as well.

You don't need to be an expert on the Bible or a trained teacher to lead a Bible discussion. The idea behind these inductive studies is that the leader guides group members to discover for themselves what the Bible has to say. This method of learning will allow group members to remember much more of what is said than a lecture would.

These studies are designed to be led easily. As a matter of fact, the flow of questions through the passage from observation to interpretation to application is so natural that you may feel that the studies lead themselves. This study guide is also flexible. You can use it with a variety of groups—student, professional, neighborhood or church groups. Each study takes forty-five to sixty minutes in a group setting.

There are some important facts to know about group dynamics and encouraging discussion. The suggestions listed below should enable you to effectively and enjoyably fulfill your role as leader.

Preparing for the Study

1. Ask God to help you understand and apply the passage in your own life. Unless this happens, you will not be prepared to lead others. Pray too for the various members of the group. Ask God to open your hearts to the message of his Word and motivate you to action.

2. Read the introduction to the entire guide to get an overview of the entire book and the issues which will be explored.

3. As you begin each study, read and reread the assigned Bible passage to familiarize yourself with it.

4. This study guide is based on the New International Version of the Bible. It will help you and the group if you use this translation as the basis for your study and discussion.

5. Carefully work through each question in the study. Spend time in meditation and reflection as you consider how to respond.

6. Write your thoughts and responses in the space provided in the study guide. This will help you to express your understanding of the passage clearly.

7. It might help to have a Bible dictionary handy. Use it to look up any unfamiliar words, names or places. (For additional help on how to study a passage, see chapter five of *Leading Bible Discussions,* InterVarsity Press.)

8. Consider how you can apply the Scripture to your life. Remember that the group will follow your lead in responding to the studies. They will not go any deeper than you do.

9. Once you have finished your own study of the passage, familiarize yourself with the leader's notes for the study you are leading. These are designed to help you in several ways. First, they tell you the purpose the study guide author had in mind when writing the study. Take time to think through how the study questions work together to accomplish that purpose. Second, the notes provide you with additional background information or suggestions on group dynamics for various questions. This information can be useful when people have difficulty understanding or answering a question. Third, the leader's notes can alert you to potential problems you may encounter during the study.

10. If you wish to remind yourself of anything mentioned in the leader's notes, make a note to yourself below that question in the study.

Leading the Study

1. Begin the study on time. Open with prayer, asking God to help the group to understand and apply the passage.

2. Be sure that everyone in your group has a study guide. Encourage the group to prepare beforehand for each discussion by reading the introduction to the guide and by working through the questions in the study.

3. At the beginning of your first time together, explain that these studies are meant to be discussions, not lectures. Encourage the members of the group to participate. However, do not put pressure on those who may be hesitant to speak during the first few sessions. You may want to suggest the fol-

lowing guidelines to your group.

☐ Stick to the topic being discussed.

☐ Your responses should be based on the verses which are the focus of the discussion and not on outside authorities such as commentaries or speakers.

☐ These studies focus on a particular passage of Scripture. Only rarely should you refer to other portions of the Bible. This allows for everyone to participate in in-depth study on equal ground.

☐ Anything said in the group is considered confidential and will not be discussed outside the group unless specific permission is given to do so.

☐ We will listen attentively to each other and provide time for each person present to talk.

☐ We will pray for each other.

4. Have a group member read the introduction at the beginning of the discussion.

5. Every session begins with a group discussion question. The question or activity is meant to be used before the passage is read. The question introduces the theme of the study and encourages group members to begin to open up. Encourage as many members as possible to participate, and be ready to get the discussion going with your own response.

This section is designed to reveal where our thoughts or feelings need to be transformed by Scripture. That is why it is especially important not to read the passage before the discussion question is asked. The passage will tend to color the honest reactions people would otherwise give because they are, of course, supposed to think the way the Bible does.

You may want to supplement the group discussion question with an icebreaker to help people to get comfortable. See the community section of *Small Group Idea Book* for more ideas.

You also might want to use the personal reflection question with your group. Either allow a time of silence for people to respond individually or discuss it together.

6. Have a group member (or members if the passage is long) read aloud the passage to be studied. Then give people several minutes to read the passage again silently so that they can take it all in.

7. Question 1 will generally be an overview question designed to briefly survey the passage. Encourage the group to look at the whole passage, but try to avoid getting sidetracked by questions or issues that will be addressed later in the study.

8. As you ask the questions, keep in mind that they are designed to be used just as they are written. You may simply read them aloud. Or you may prefer to express them in your own words.

There may be times when it is appropriate to deviate from the study guide. For example, a question may have already been answered. If so, move on to the next question. Or someone may raise an important question not covered in the guide. Take time to discuss it, but try to keep the group from going off on tangents.

9. Avoid answering your own questions. If necessary, repeat or rephrase them until they are clearly understood. Or point out something you read in the leader's notes to clarify the context or meaning. An eager group quickly becomes passive and silent if they think the leader will do most of the talking.

10. Don't be afraid of silence. People may need time to think about the question before formulating their answers.

11. Don't be content with just one answer. Ask, "What do the rest of you think?" or "Anything else?" until several people have given answers to the question.

12. Acknowledge all contributions. Try to be affirming whenever possible. Never reject an answer. If it is clearly off-base, ask, "Which verse led you to that conclusion?" or again, "What do the rest of you think?"

13. Don't expect every answer to be addressed to you, even though this will probably happen at first. As group members become more at ease, they will begin to truly interact with each other. This is one sign of healthy discussion.

14. Don't be afraid of controversy. It can be very stimulating. If you don't resolve an issue completely, don't be frustrated. Move on and keep it in mind for later. A subsequent study may solve the problem.

15. Periodically summarize what the group has said about the passage. This helps to draw together the various ideas mentioned and gives continuity to the study. But don't preach.

16. At the end of the Bible discussion you may want to allow group members a time of quiet to work on an idea under "Now or Later." Then discuss what you experienced. Or you may want to encourage group members to work on these ideas between meetings. Give an opportunity during the session for people to talk about what they are learning.

17. Conclude your time together with conversational prayer, adapting the prayer suggestion at the end of the study to your group. Ask for God's help in following through on the commitments you've made.

18. End on time.

Many more suggestions and helps are found in *Leading Bible Discussions,* which is part of the LifeGuide Bible Study series.

Components of Small Groups
A healthy small group should do more than study the Bible. There are four components to consider as you structure your time together.

Nurture. Small groups help us to grow in our knowledge and love of God. Bible study is the key to making this happen and is the foundation of your small group.

Community. Small groups are a great place to develop deep friendships with other Christians. Allow time for informal interaction before and after each study. Plan activities and games that will help you get to know each other. Spend time having fun together—going on a picnic or cooking dinner together.

Worship and prayer. Your study will be enhanced by spending time praising God together in prayer or song. Pray for each other's needs—and keep track of how God is answering prayer in your group. Ask God to help you to apply what you are learning in your study.

Outreach. Reaching out to others can be a practical way of applying what you are learning, and it will keep your group from becoming self-focused. Host a series of evangelistic discussions for your friends or neighbors. Clean up the yard of an elderly friend. Serve at a soup kitchen together, or spend a day working on a Habitat house.

Many more suggestions and helps in each of these areas are found in *Small Group Idea Book.* Information on building a small group can be found in *Small Group Leaders' Handbook* and *The Big Book on Small Groups* (both from InterVarsity Press). Reading through one of these books would be worth your time.

General note. It is important that you work through the questions in each study from beginning to end. The questions were written to help you discover Matthew's main point. If only half the questions for a study are covered, it will be difficult to understand what Matthew intends to convey. In order to cover the questions in a 45 to 55 minute study, firm leadership is very important. The leader will need to keep the group moving and not allow people to fix on any one question for too long.

Part 1: Discovering the King.
Study 1. Matthew 1—2. In Search of the King.
Purpose: To show that Jesus came as the heavenly king and that everyone must respond to him—either worship him or reject him.
Question 1. It is clear that Matthew is not giving an exhaustive genealogy. He is more interested in showing significant relationships. The lineage is impor-

tant for several reasons. First, it establishes Jesus' royal lineage as the rightful king of Israel. Second, it shows his Jewish lineage (contrasted with Herod who was only half Jewish and not of a royal line). Third, the lineage shows how Jesus fulfills prophecy as the anointed king sent from God.

Notice that several women are mentioned in the lineage. In light of the Great Commission at the end of the book it is significant that several of the women were not of Jewish descent. Being a son of David, Jesus is qualified to be the Jewish king. As a son of Abraham, Jesus is indisputably Jewish.

Question 3. The contrasts between Jesus and Herod are striking. Jesus was completely Jewish; Herod was of a mixed race. Jesus was sent by God; Herod was placed on the throne by the Romans. Jesus was to be shepherd of Israel; Herod was an exploiter of Israel. Herod took the lives of children to keep his throne; Jesus gave up his life so that the throne might be given to him. Herod "occupied" the Jewish capital; Jesus was born in King David's city.

Question 4. There are many legends about the Magi; in later church tradition they are even given names. Study of the ancient Near-Eastern culture suggests that they were astrologers who attempted to tell the future by looking at the stars. However, from this passage there is not a great deal that we know about them. What is important to note is that these foreigners are able to find out about his birth and come to celebrate him, thus establishing that Jesus' birth has international significance.

Question 6. Help group members recall ways in which an interest in God has affected the books they have read, the friends they have chosen, the church they attend.

Question 8. Jesus is not welcomed by the established authorities of the Jewish world, but he is welcomed by the foreign Magi. The religious leaders did not seek out the place of Jesus' birth and were not looking to welcome him.

Question 9. Herod was the first of many authority figures who wished to put Jesus to death. Not being a full-blooded Jew, he had reason to fear one "born King of the Jews."

Question 11. Someone once said, "God is obvious by his absence, and his silence is the loudest noise in the universe." In this passage God is active in every single thing that happens, but he is seldom mentioned.

Question 12. In the book of Revelation worshiping the Lamb on the throne is the central activity of heaven. How fitting that the worship of Christ begins the moment of his birth. We can gain insight into our spiritual health by considering whether there is a worshipful tone in our thoughts, attitudes and actions.

Now or Later. Suggest that people complete this material on their own during the week or take a session to go through it together. You will want to do this section prior to study 1 if you do it as a separate session. These questions survey Matthew's material and style and help the group catch a glimpse of his purpose. Don't be overwhelmed by the material they will cover. Skim each page while looking for the obvious. In-depth study will come later.

Question 3. Matthew's theme is discipleship. He records Jesus' command to make disciples of the nations, "teaching them to obey everything I have commanded you." He gives us, in his Gospel, commands and other important information that are necessary to make disciples. He, more than any other Gospel writer, gives us the content of what Jesus taught.

Question 5. Matthew also wants us to see Jesus as the heavenly King who rules over us. Beginning in Matthew 2 there is a repeated emphasis on kingship, the royal of authority of Jesus. Also unique to Matthew is the emphasis on the kingdom of heaven as opposed to the kingdom of God, which is recorded by Mark and Luke. Matthew helps us see that Jesus' spiritual authority is supreme in all areas of life.

Question 8. Some Christians think of conversion only as a decision at a specific point in time. Think about the process by which God brought you into a life of discipleship.

Study 2. Matthew 3. Preparing for the King.

Purpose: To see that in order to receive the King we must prepare our hearts and be willing to turn from sin.

Question 1. John's ministry was modeled after Elijah's. In 2 Kings 1:8 Elijah is described as wearing a garment of hair and a leather belt around his waist. In Malachi 4:5 the one who is to prepare the way for the coming Lord is the prophet Elijah.

Question 2. Israel wandered for forty years in the desert because of unbelief. Yet it was in the desert that they learned to trust God enough to follow him into the Promised Land. Ministering in the desert, John the Baptist delivers judgment on the unbelieving religious leaders and offers the blessings of forgiveness to those who felt their need.

Question 3. To be a child of Abraham meant that one belonged to God and the promises of the covenant. Evidently the religious leaders were depending upon their heritage for their relationship with God instead of cultivating a personal knowledge of God.

Question 4. Help people consider whether they may be depending on their religious affiliation or some previous commitment that they might have made to the Lord. God wants a present and vital relationship with each of us.

Question 6. While John's baptism of water was outward and symbolic, Jesus' baptism was one of actual power. It brings judgment on the unrepentant and a harvest of blessing to the responsive.

Question 7. John knew that his baptism was a form of divine judgment opening a door of divine forgiveness. John had trouble with the idea of bringing a baptism of judgment on God's righteous Messiah.

Question 8. Jesus' willingness to receive baptism at the hands of John displayed his willingness to identify with the sins of the Jewish nation and to receive judgment from God. At the outset of his ministry it foreshadows the cross as the means by which he would fulfill his mission.

Question 9. The entire Trinity is involved at this crucial beginning point of Jesus' ministry.

Question 10. The mystery of the kingdom of heaven is that the Christ who has come is coming again. We need to examine our life to see that it is bearing fruit and not chaff.

Study 3. Matthew 4. The Beginning of the Kingdom.

Purpose: To catch the excitement of being invited to join Jesus' compassionate and powerful kingdom.

Question 1. Refer to a map of Israel. Zebulon, Napthali and Galilee are in northern Israel; Syria and Decapolis are beyond the borders of Israel; Jerusalem and Judea are in southern Israel.

Question 2. Satan seems to be questioning Jesus' identity as the Son of God. Notice the repetition of the word *if* in verses 6 and 7. Everything revolved around the identity of Jesus as the Son of God. If Jesus doubted he was the Son of God, then he was not a threat to Satan. Jesus would merely have been another miracle worker or aspiring messianic revolutionary.

Question 3. Commentators have noticed that Jesus was tempted in areas of humanity's greatest needs: sustenance, security and significance. Jesus was unshakable in his sense of identity and his sense of mission, and he was not interested in proving anything to Satan.

Question 4. Jesus was not even open to a "conversation" about the issues. Unlike Adam and Eve, who were drawn into a dialogue about what God had and hadn't said, Jesus counters Satan's use of Scripture by quoting Scripture back to him. We can learn from this and not allow ourselves to be drawn in to diabolical debates and doubts. For us and for Jesus Scripture is the safe place to stand and the only safe thing to say in response to the evil one.

Question 5. Jesus is to be a light to the Gentiles, again foreshadowing the Great Commission. His ministry is one of preaching. The essence of Jesus' message is repentance in preparation for the kingdom of heaven. In contrast Mark and Luke write of the kingdom of God. This difference has puzzled commentators for centuries. Our suggestion is that Matthew wanted to emphasize that Jesus' kingdom was of a spiritual nature and would continue after he ascended to heaven. Jesus rules us on earth from his heavenly throne.

Question 6. A kingdom consists of a king with authority, subjects he rules over and the power to defend his realm. In these verses we see Jesus as an authority figure who calls followers (citizens) and delivers his people from sickness and evil spirits. He is portrayed as the king from heaven who brings healing, compassion and deliverance.

Question 7. This is a key concept, central to the book of Matthew. Discipleship means following Jesus Christ. This simple definition needs to be considered closely. First, discipleship is personal—it is being in a relationship with the person Jesus Christ. We are not called into a program of instruction. Second, the relationship with Jesus takes priority over everything else—family, vocation and so on. Third, discipleship produces a transformation. Jesus promised to redirect the disciples from fishing for fish to fishing for people. Fourth, discipleship has a mission focus. He requires that we learn to care for others so that we can reach out to bring others into a discipleship relationship.

Study 4. Matthew 5:1—6:18. The Law of the King (Part 1).
Purpose: To learn how the law of Jesus reaches into our hearts and requires total obedience.

Group Discussion. You will need to allow fifteen to twenty minutes for this activity. It is designed to introduce the topic but can also help you to make some changes in your group. You may want to focus the topic a bit, depending on what area of group life you need to fine tune.

Question 3. The first four beatitudes seem to concern people who have a need: the poor, who have no resources; those who mourn, who face a loss of some kind; the meek, who have no influence; those who hunger and thirst for righteousness, who have a need for holiness. In God's kingdom, however, those without resource inherit the kingdom. Those who are mourning also have comfort. Those with no influence gain the entire land. Those who lack righteousness are freely given it.

Three of the remaining four beatitudes deal with conflicts between people: The merciful show kindness toward the undeserving, the peacemakers seek to resolve conflict, and those who are persecuted suffer oppression. In his kingdom his disciples receive mercy because they have given it, receive the source of mercy—the sight of God—and receive the heavenly kingdom because they have been rejected from the earthly one.

Some commentators suggest that the Beatitudes should be qualities not only of each disciple but of the messianic community. Churches composed of such qualities would be not only meeting places in which one attended once or twice a week but a counterculture pointing to heavenly realities.

Question 4. The images of salt and light continue the theme of discipleship having an impact on others. It is important to note that the effect on society is the result of disciples who possess the qualities set forth in the Beatitudes.

Question 5. Jesus' ministry will include a direct assault on the religious leaders and their Scripture-twisting system. As Jesus lays down the platform for his kingdom, he makes it clear that his ministry is based on Scripture and, in contrast to the religious system, is faithful to God's purposes for the law.

Question 9. Jesus forgives sin, but he never excuses it. A righteous God cannot say, "A little bit of sin is acceptable." God's standard for his disciples is righteousness and purity. And as Jesus has just shown by his teaching, God's Law goes past outward actions and straight to the heart.

Question 10. The contrasts continue in chapter 6, but there the focus is not on traditions and the Law but on motives and "acts of righteousness."

Question 11. The inner life is one of the main themes of the kingdom of heaven clearly seen in the Sermon on the Mount. It is "heart responses" that God is concerned with.

Question 12. Jesus has high expectations of us. There is a sense of "firmness" in his character that comes out in the Sermon. Jesus also displays insight into human behavior; he knows what motivates us.

Study 5. Matthew 6:19—7:29. The Law of the King (Part 2).

Purpose: To count the cost and blessings of obeying the King's laws.

Question 1. The issue here, as in much of the Sermon on the Mount (and, for that matter, the kingdom of heaven), is one of motives and inner desires. It is worth noting that Jesus' teaching is a direct challenge to the modern worldview that places a high priority on the horizontal dimension of life. We are concerned with the here and now. It requires a conversion of both heart and mind to see the vertical dimension of heavenly treasures as a significant motivator.

Question 2. The Old English word for worry meant "to gnaw at the neck like a wolf chewing on its prey." Note that Jesus is not saying that we shouldn't give consideration to our food and clothing. He is saying that we should not worry about them. Anxiety about earthly consideration is contrary to the kingdom of heaven because eternal issues are the priority and bring with them earthly blessings.

Question 4. The requirement to seek God's kingdom first is an application of the first commandment: "You shall have no other gods before me." It is human nature to make God our servant and give personal concerns the priority. This is not the converted, repentant way of a citizen of the kingdom. Everything is second to God, even the most basic issues of sustenance. It is not that these are unimportant but that eternal concerns bring with them temporal blessings.

Question 5. Judgment implies legal authority to decide a person's guilt or innocence. When we "judge" others we are rendering a decision about how righteous or unrighteous they are. This is a prerogative that belongs only to God. In discernment we are not rendering a legal judgment. Discernment is understanding the present disposition of others toward us and acting accordingly.

Questions 6-7. The Christian church over the past 2,000 years has splintered into thousands of independent groups for many reasons. Behind many doctrinal disagreements hides a sense of self-righteousness that judges others. The Christian community is intended to be a safe place in which grace, not judgment, is extended by citizens to one another.

Question 8. Although Jesus' words about seeking, asking and knocking can be applied in general to prayer, in their specific context Jesus is teaching that prayer is necessary to receive the resources to live by the demands of laws of his kingdom.

Question 10. Following the king is a matter of the heart, a converted heart that places God first. Although God alone can see the heart, given enough time, the heart always shows itself for what it is. Jesus teaches that we are not to judge each other, but we must be alert to false prophets with false hearts, which can be unmasked by the fruit they bear.

Study 6. Matthew 8:1—9:34. The Powers of the King.

Purpose: To see the power of the King and to learn to please him by growing in faith.

Background. These two chapters are a collection of the miracles that Jesus accomplished. Matthew has concentrated the majority of the miracles that he records in these two chapters. For these reasons they form a unity. Matthew has organized the miracles to show that Jesus, the king of the kingdom of heaven, has authority over everything and everyone.

Along with the theme of miracles is the theme of faith. The word *faith* is used repeatedly in these two chapters. Faith is the proper response to the authority of the King. Faith allows us to receive his authority and opens the knowledge of the kingdom to us.

Question 2. This incident displays the power and compassion of Jesus. Lepers were excluded from all social contact. The man is obviously desperate, for he violates Jewish laws to approach Jesus in the midst of a crowd. To touch a leper in Jewish society was to become unclean. However, when Jesus touched the leprous man, instead of becoming unclean he made the leprous man clean.

Question 4. Jesus commends the centurion because, having only heard of Jesus, he was able to discern both Jesus' goodness and his power and to believe that Jesus could heal from a distance. By faith we can seek Jesus for all kinds of needs, trusting that he will indeed meet them if we ask.

Question 5. Jesus is not desperate for followers. He accepts only those who are willing to pay the high price of placing him above everything else.

Question 6. The fury of the storm and the depth of their fear is evident when we consider that the disciples were seasoned fishermen and had sailed on the lake all their lives. The disciples' fear of the storm stands in contrast to the faith of the centurion. The disciples were not able to trust Jesus' power over something they had never experienced before. Jesus wants the disciples to trust him completely. They have not yet arrived at this depth of spiritual insight, yet Jesus keeps the expectation high.

Questions 8-9. Jesus' display of power over the violent men was terrifying, and sending the pigs into the water seriously damaged the townspeople's economy. Jesus was not comfortable to have around. He intruded on established ways of living and believing. Those who were comfortable with the status quo found Jesus threatening.

Question 10. As a doctor Jesus brings spiritual health to those sick with sin. As a bridegroom he brings celebration to those who love him. The parables of wine and new cloth means that he can't be understood if he is limited to old traditions and worn out expectations. The emphasis is on distinctiveness. The kingdom Jesus brings is new and distinct. His ministry cannot be patched onto old traditions or contained by traditional restraints (vv. 6-17). Jesus sets himself as the standard for fasting, feasting or any other activity. If he is present, there is no need to fast, no matter what the custom. What Matthew wants us to see is that Jesus can't be placed within normal human expectations. Jesus is the standard by which everything is measured, and he will not accept measurement according to any human standard.

Study 7. Matthew 9:35—11:30. The Messengers of the King.

Purpose: To see that we must count both the cost and the blessings of being the King's messengers.

General note. Remember that the theme of discipleship runs throughout Matthew. In this section we see the disciples being transformed into fishers of people. Jesus has modeled the ministry of the kingdom and now sends them out to put into practice what they have learned from him.

Question 2. The disciples are being sent out as representatives of the kingdom of heaven. The peace that they will offer to people is not just a wish for well-being and good fortune. Rather, it is the gift of spiritual peace and right standing in the sight of heaven. The rejection of the peace the disciples offer is serious and has eternal consequences. For this reason it was important that the disciples physically displayed the consequences of their actions by shaking the dust off their feet in response to rejection.

Jesus' instructions at this point are directed at Israel. The disciples function as royal heralds proclaiming the coming of the messianic King.

Question 4. Jesus' ministry is full of confusing tensions. His ability to heal and teach was definitely attractive to the crowds. However, his uncompromising demand to be first in the lives of his disciples was threatening. Especially for those who were comfortable with the status quo, Jesus and his disciples would not be welcome.

Question 5. The central issue in discipleship is the priority of Jesus. Remember that the disciples had to leave their families and vocations in order to follow the Lord. Those who follow Jesus must be willing to experience conflict even within the family because eternal concerns about an eternal God vastly outweigh family problems.

Chapter 11 continues a theme that began in chapter ten. We see the consequences of those that have heard Jesus' message and refused to respond.

Question 6. While John was responsive to and had prepared the way for Jesus, his faith was wavering. Jesus was not meeting John's expectations of the Messiah. After all, John was still in prison when he expected to be delivered by the conquering Messiah. Jesus offered concrete evidence that he was in fact the Messiah and performed messianic acts as prophesied in Isaiah 61.

Question 9. Jesus' denunciations must be seen in light of the mission of the twelve disciples. They had gone throughout the nation proclaiming the kingdom, healing people and casting out demons. Despite both Jesus' and the disciples' ministry, people in those cities still refused to believe.

Study 8. Matthew 12. The Leaders & the King.

Purpose: To feel the security of belonging to the King as we see Jesus handle opposition with wisdom and power.

General note. The opposition to Jesus that has been slowly building now becomes open conflict. As the religious leaders seek to oppose him, Jesus confronts them with the serious consequences of their actions.

Question 3. If the religious establishment could demonstrate that the Law supported their teaching, then they could prove that Jesus was not sent from God. On the other hand if Jesus could demonstrate that they had not understood the Law correctly, then his authority would be established and the religious leaders discredited. Meeting personal needs and service to God are not forbidden on the sabbath. Implicit in Jesus' answer is the claim of his own divinity. The disciples were with him and doing his will.

Question 4. Instead of hearing the religious leaders of Jesus' time saying, "Look at what your disciples are doing," today we hear, "Look at what the church has done." The Spirit of God continues to call by pointing us toward Jesus himself. This is precisely what fallen humanity avoids.

Question 5. While Jesus is healing people on the sabbath, the religious leaders are plotting his murder.

Question 6. This question is an invitation to acknowledge that the church is not perfect and neither are the leaders God works through. Many have been hurt by spiritual authorities who have misused what God has entrusted in them. There is always a danger that spiritual leaders will take ownership of God's grace as if it were their own. The result is that others are hurt or abused in some way.

Question 8. The accusation that Jesus served Satan was the second prong of the Pharisees' attack on Jesus. If the Pharisees could convince people that Jesus was demonic, then everything he did and taught would be considered evil. The sin against the Holy Spirit is unforgivable because it is a choice of darkness and a hard heart. It is the Spirit that brings light and a responsive heart. When we call the work of the Holy Spirit evil, then there is no avenue left open for God to work in us. By attributing the work of Jesus to the evil spirit as opposed to the Holy Spirit, the religious leaders were putting themselves in danger of complete darkness.

Question 10. The extent of evil that the religious leaders are committing is illustrated as Jesus compares them with Gentiles who were willing to repent when confronted with God's judgment.

Study 9. Matthew 13. The Parables of the King.

Purpose: To learn that only through sincere interest can we understand the mystery of Jesus' kingdom.

Background. There are a variety of definitions of a parable and explanations for how to interpret one. For our purposes we will define a parable as a story that illustrates the message of the kingdom of heaven. This is a lot of material to cover in one study, but there are benefits from doing so. When we look at all the parables here in one setting, we can begin to see the common theme of the growth of the kingdom of heaven.

Studying the parables requires sober judgment. Many people are inclined to become fanciful in their interpretations. The best way to avoid error when studying parables is to look for the main point. Then consider how Jesus' teaching would be understood by those to whom he was speaking. Check to see if the interpretation fits with the questions being asked and with the issues under consideration.

Question 2. Remember, the theme of Jesus' message was that the kingdom of heaven is at hand. This message could be paraphrased to say that Jesus, the One sent from heaven, is here to bring God's rule. The parables illustrate the way the authority of Jesus is active in the world.

Question 3. Don't allow the discussion of this parable to be sidetracked with the question of "eternal security." The issue is not whether everyone who responds to the preaching of the Word is eternally secure. Rather it is that there are a variety of responses to the gospel, not all of which are truly genuine. This parable is frequently called "the parable of the sower." It could easily be called "the parable of the soils." The difference between responses is the varying quality of the soil. Following the continued emphasis on the inner responses to Jesus in the Gospel of Matthew, it is possible to look at the quality of the soils as the quality of our hearts as they respond to Jesus' message.

The opposition to growth could be described as "the world, the flesh and the devil." The devil takes up the seed from the heart, the flesh does not persevere in times of tribulation and the world creates such temptation that the seed becomes choked.

Question 4. Remember that Jesus is now speaking to a crowd that has been infected with opposition from the religious leaders. Jesus must now teach in such a way as to elicit the interest of those who are spiritually hungry but confused by the false teaching about him. The mystery of a parable is revealed to those who are interested enough to ask questions when they don't understand. It is hidden from those who are not spiritually interested and hungry.

Question 5. One of the reasons that the kingdom of heaven is mysterious is because of the way it grows. Until the end of the age it has a mixed character. Not everyone who appears to be a member of the kingdom really is. Who really is and is not a member of the kingdom will not be made known until the consummation of the kingdom at Christ's second coming.

This is not a parable that forbids church discipline, as some might imagine. The field is the world, not the church. Those who might prematurely pull up weeds are not other Christians ("sons of the kingdom") but the divine servants, probably angels.

Question 6. The kingdom of heaven is also mysterious because of the way it begins. It started much smaller than expected. Instead of coming in with a conquering army, Jesus chose twelve disciples. And instead of setting up a separate political order, he has sent his disciples as salt in the world or as yeast working throughout the dough.

Study 10. Matthew 14. The Revelation of the King.
Purpose: To see how Jesus uses our experience to bring disciples to spiritual insight.

Question 1. Herod had been hearing about the works of Jesus. This question affords an opportunity to reflect on what Matthew has told about the mighty works of Jesus up to this point, particularly of chapters 8 and 9.

Question 2. St. Augustine, reflecting on the first sin and the Fall of Adam and Eve, speculated that at the root of all sin is a fear of what others, rather than God, might think about us. The murder of John the Baptist by Herod would certainly confirm the fear of others as a source of disobedience and sin. Peer pressure then is not merely a problem of adolescence, it is a human problem that we all must struggle with all of our lives.

Question 4. Again, this question must be answered in light of the previous study of Matthew. The disciples are called to exercise faith based on all that they have learned from being with Jesus and through ministering in his name. Faith requires that we take risks based on the character and the power of our Lord. Knowing that John's death at the hands of Herod was a foreshadowing of his own, Jesus steps up his training of the disciples.

Question 5. Herod's banquet shows that he is afraid of others. He revels in drunken debauchery and feeds others from the public treasury. Jesus shows a concern for others and demonstrates that he is able to multiply meager resources to meet the needs of those who come to him.

Question 8. The significance of the disciples' confession can only be understood against the background of their Jewish heritage. God's holiness was so jealously protected that many refused even to pronounce God's name. Although the disciples don't yet see Jesus for who he truly is, the fact that they worshiped him shows that they are growing close to that essential spiritual insight. Following the disciples' example the worship of Jesus always comes from spiritual insight and leads to deeper spiritual insight.

Study 11. Matthew 15:1—16:20. Understanding the King.

Purpose: To see that our understanding the identity of Jesus is the central issue of the kingdom of heaven.

General note. This is another long study. The reason that there is so much material to cover in one study is that Matthew is giving crucial details that lead up to the great confession of Peter. A central theme as you work through this material is that of insight. Jesus wanted his disciples to look into the works he had done to see the true meaning of the kingdom of heaven.

Question 1. The escalating conflict with the religious leaders continues in these two chapters. At this point the issue of who really is faithful to the law is settled. The tradition of Corban, allowing someone to declare money or a piece of property as devoted to the God and then given as gift to be used in the temple, appeared holy. In reality it allowed people to avoid family obligations for religious advancement and social prestige.

Question 2. The issue of the heart, which has been implicitly touched on throughout the ministry of Jesus, is now stated explicitly. The discussion of the quality of the heart sets up the disciples for revelation of his identity as the Christ, the Son of God, in chapter 16.

Question 5. The central issue of these chapters is the issue of insight, looking past outward acts to the truth. This Gentile woman approached Jesus as the Jewish king, the "Son of David." She receives help from Jesus when she moves past the apparent rejection. Seeing her faith and insight, Jesus grants her request. Matthew records this incident to show us that Jesus would expect the same insight from his disciples.

Question 6. Jesus refuses to give a sign because the religious leaders were too blind to see the true meaning of his works. In effect, it was not possible to receive a sign from heaven.

Question 7. The disciples look only at the outward and obvious meaning of Jesus. This was the problem of the religious leaders.

Question 8. Peter is given spiritual insight by divine revelation from the Father. The faith to perceive that Jesus is the Christ, the Son of God, is not natural, it's supernatural.

Question 11. These verses about locking and unlocking the kingdom are known as "the keys to the kingdom." The Christian community, represented by Peter, is central to the proclamation of the gospel and the means of eternal life. Using a parabolic style, Jesus teaches that the confession of his identity is the central issue of both heaven and earth.

Part 2: The Rejection & Resurrection of the King.
Study 12. Matthew 16:21—17:27. The Work of the King.
Purpose: To learn that living by faith means that we may not always understand; nevertheless, we must trust and obey.

Question 1. This statement must have been hard for the disciples to believe, for several reasons. First, it would be unthinkable that the Messiah should die before establishing his kingdom. Second, it would be incomprehensible that the religious leaders, as opposed to Jesus as they may have been, could actually kill God's Messiah. (It is ironic that Jesus' enemies are the leaders of Israel rather than the heathen oppressors.)

Question 3. It is possible that Satan was speaking through Peter. Or it may be that Jesus used Satan as a figure of speech to show the terrible implications of trying to revise the true purpose of his mission.

Question 4. Jesus reveals the true cost of discipleship. Not only must we place him first by leaving everything, as in 4:18ff; 10:37ff. But we must place our own lives in his hands as well. The cross is an instrument of death, like a hanging noose in the Old West. Jesus is saying that we must be ready to die, even to the point of carrying our own rope so that we can be hanged!

Question 6. "Son of Man" refers to a bright, shining figure in Daniel 7:14 who comes from heaven at the end of times to judge the nations and set up a kingdom that will never be destroyed. The mystery of the kingdom of heaven is that it is present in the person of Jesus. When the disciples see Jesus revealed in all his glory as the Son of Man, they are seeing Jesus as he truly is, the King of the kingdom of heaven. In light of Jesus' shattering prediction of his death, it was important for them to know that death was not the end.

Question 7. Moses and Elijah may represent the two major divisions of the Old Testament: the Law and the Prophets. God appeared to Israel in a cloud as he led the nation through the wilderness.

Question 9. Malachi prophesied that Elijah would return before the final judgment. Jesus sees a present and a future role for Elijah, preceding both Jesus' first and second comings.

Now or Later. These questions, like those at the end of the first part of this guide, are intended to help you survey the main themes. Don't be overwhelmed by the amount of material that will be covered. Remember to skim and page flip. Look for obvious points.

In this survey you will see a continued escalation of the conflict and tension between Jesus and the religious leaders. The cross that Jesus declares to

Peter in Matthew 16:21 is discernible just behind the scenes in each chapter. Along with the increase in tension between Jesus and the religious leaders is the continued instruction of the disciples. Another theme that continues to build in this half of Matthew is the authority of Jesus. Much of the action takes place in Jerusalem, from chapter 21 onward, in and around the temple. If we have eyes to see, he is the King in his capital city that is controlled by rebels. The final victory of the King comes not as he expels the rebels but as he submits to them, is killed and is raised to life by the Father. In the final earthly scene (Mt 28), he announces that the kingdom of heaven is indeed at hand and that all authority in heaven and on earth has been given to him.

Study 13. Matthew 18. The Greatest in the Kingdom.

Purpose: To discover some of the values Jesus requires as we live in his kingdom.

General note. Jesus continues his instruction of his disciples. There are similarities between this material and the Sermon on the Mount. In the Sermon on the Mount, Jesus instructs the disciples of the essentials of discipleship as they have just begun to follow him. In chapters 18-20 Jesus is instructing them in discipleship as he prepares to physically leave them. He is telling them what they will need to know in order to lead the church. The central theme of the three chapters is "Who is the greatest in the kingdom of heaven?" It begins in 18:1 and continues through 20:28 when the mother of James and John request positions of honor for them.

Question 1. Concerning the topic of children, most people assume that Jesus is encouraging trust, openness and innocence. However, the main point concerning children is that they have little social status; we don't naturally think of children as being "great." Jesus teaches that positions of greatness in the kingdom are not to be calculated according to traditional understanding of social status.

Question 4. Answer this in light of Matthew's teaching about disciplemaking. We will be held accountable for the quality of lives and the influence of our teaching. Remember Jesus' teaching in the Sermon on the Mount, we are to be perfect as our Father in heaven is perfect. Jesus is serious about sin, it is internally and externally destructive. He never says or implies that a little bit of sin is okay. The ultimate cost of sin is not merely an eye or a hand but his life sacrificed on the cross. It is imperative then as his disciples that we live lives of purity and integrity.

Question 5. This also addresses the issue of making disciples. God wants to bring lost sheep to himself. Disciples who are following the Lord will share his concern for those who are lost.

Question 7. Quality relationships are a central issue in the kingdom of heaven. Jesus provides ways for us to handle our conflicts with one another and resolve them.

Question 10. Henri Nouwen wrote that Christians should be more concerned with "downward mobility" rather than "upward mobility." Such humility is sustainable only if we truly understand that dignity and identity come not from what we achieve or what others think about us but from our radical allegiance to Jesus Christ.

Study 14. Matthew 19—20. Life in the Kingdom.

Purpose: To discover some of the values Jesus requires as we live in his kingdom.

Question 1. Attitudes toward divorce in the culture of that time, while not as casual as in the modern world, were not nearly as firm as that which Jesus advocates. A wife was looked upon as property that could be disposed of if her husband was dissatisfied with her.

Question 2. Both singleness and marriage in the kingdom of heaven require supernatural grace being lived out. They require commitment, faithfulness, forgiveness, humility and submission to God.

Question 3. The way of life in the kingdom of heaven is counterintuitive. It is not at all the way we naturally conceive of living.

Question 4. We are to live expectantly, looking forward to the abundant and eternal provisions of the kingdom. Our present earthly position may not correspond to our future eternal position (19:30).

Question 7. God is free to give us what he chooses; he owes us nothing for any of our labor. Any amount he pays us is an expression of grace.

Question 8. Jesus graciously gives to those who ask. He serves those who he has no obligation to help. (Remember, the "little ones" are important in the kingdom.)

Question 9. There is nothing wrong with wanting to be great. There is something wrong with wanting to be first. "First" implies that someone gets ahead of someone else. This comparative social competition is the very thing Jesus despises. The way to greatness in the kingdom is humility. To be by Jesus' side means service to the needy, not exaltation in public ceremonies in the exercise of raw power.

Study 15. Matthew 21:1-27. The King Occupies His Capital.

Purpose: To observe the rising conflict in Jerusalem over Jesus' authority and to reflect on what Jesus expects of his subjects.

Question 3. Some saw Jesus as the king who would free the Jewish nation from oppression and then rule over them forever. Others saw Jesus as a prophet. However, a Jewish person would not equate the Son of David with a prophet.

Question 4. Public celebrations are great tools to draw us into worship and praise. The crowd was giving to Christ the glory due him. In their case it was with little understanding and no heart allegiance.

Question 5. The central issue is the authority of Jesus. As Jesus enters Jerusalem, the conflict between him and the religious leaders reaches a boiling point. The temple was the center of the Jewish religious system. This act was the ultimate assault on Jewish identity and therefore intolerable. It was inevitable after his clearing out the temple that the leadership would move swiftly to eradicate him.

For Jesus too the temple was a central issue. The King sent to bring the rule of heaven goes to the temple where he should receive the prayer and praise of God's people. Instead he must drive out those who are busy making a worldly profit.

Question 6. The temple was to be a place of compassion and health for the needy and a place of praise and prayer toward God. What a wonderful picture of the kingdom of heaven, children and the poor and needy streaming to the King in his capital, receiving all that they need.

Question 7. Jesus was looking for the fruit of prayer and faith. He curses the fig tree to illustrate to the disciples what the true condition of Israel is like. Israel is on the brink of withering because of their rejection of him.

What is required of the disciples is that they learn the relationship of prayer and faith. Jesus instructs the disciples on faith because that is the central issue in the conflict. The religious leaders refuse to believe and their place of worship has degenerated into a place of commerce.

The mountain that Jesus speaks of moving is not literal, of course. It is a metaphor for overcoming obstacles to the kingdom of heaven by means of prayer.

Question 8. Remember that the religious leaders have been spreading rumors that Jesus is a law-breaker and gets his power from Satan (Mt 12). They are no longer trying to discredit him with the crowds as had been their previous tactic. They are looking for ways to trap him and bring him to trial.

The underlying issue is who is right and who has the right to be in charge. If Jesus is right, then the religious leaders are no longer in power. If they are right, then Jesus is a heretical usurper who must be destroyed.

Study 16. Matthew 21:28—22:46. The King Silences the Opposition.
Purpose: To consider the dangers of rejecting Jesus' invitations.
Question 2. The conflict between Jesus and the religious leaders continues. However, instead of rejecting and avoiding them, he continues to meet with them and reach out to them in their blindness through hard-hitting parables. As we observe Jesus in this conflict, we can learn more about the character of our Lord and what he requires of us as his disciples.
Question 3. It is always good to examine our responsiveness to the Lord. Remember that the religious leaders had convinced themselves that they were doing God's will. We can have a look at our hearts by observing our actions. Are we doing what God has asked us to do, or are we merely giving lip service?
Question 4. Among other charges, Jesus is accusing the religious leaders of being guilty of his own death. Sometimes Jesus told parables to make people ponder a point and search out its meaning. In this parable and others in this passage, Jesus tells parables for dramatic effect so his opponents will feel and see the underlying motives in rejecting him.
Question 5. Again, the point is made with dramatic effect that their resistance to him means they will be excluded from God's kingdom.
Question 6. Jesus is saying, "I am with God and have his authority. You are not with God and you have no authority."
Question 7. If Jesus said they should not pay taxes, he would side with the Pharisees. If he said they should pay taxes, he would side with the Herodians.
Question 8. Resurrection was a hot topic in Jesus' day. The Pharisees argued for resurrection; the Sadducees argued against it. Jesus shows that he is master of Scripture as well as debate. He appeals to the Scriptures with an argument that is shocking in its clarity and its originality. God is not the God of Abraham who was and is no more, but the God of Abraham who is and still lives on the other side of death.
Question 10. In this paragraph we glimpse the mystery of the kingdom of heaven. Christ is both eternal and yet born. He is a son of David and yet the Lord of David. He is born in time but above time.
Question 13. Jesus does not bow to opposition out of weakness. We can trust him to protect us and draw strength from his strength.

Study 17. Matthew 23. The King Condemns the Rebels.
Purpose: To consider the commands and demands that Jesus issues to opponents and followers.
Question 1. In this chapter Jesus delivers the final judgment on the religious

leaders. There are seven woes. The number 7 has biblical significance; it means "complete and full." After this chapter, Jesus will have nothing more to say to the religious leaders. Their rejection of Jesus is total and his condemnation of them is delivered.

Question 3. Jesus is not against spiritual authority in general. He is against the spiritual leaders of this generation who have used authority to satisfy their own lust for power.

Questions 4-5. Jesus admonished his disciples to be aware of the yeast of the Pharisees and Sadducees. Their yeast had worked its way into their hearts and puffed them up with a love of power and prestige. It was a desire to be "first" and "greatest." Jesus teaches his disciples that they must not aspire to be spiritual authorities, but servants who teach with humility, knowing their place and staying in it.

Question 7. It is helpful to look at the woes to get a feel for the significance of what Jesus is saying. Notice the condemnation for ignoring the intent of the Law and being concerned about outward righteousness. These are significant in light of the importance of inner motives for the disciples of the kingdom of heaven. As you look over the woes, remember that this is more than just an emotional outburst. This is the final word of the King personally delivered to the rebels.

Question 8. Think of ways that personal acts of piety can degenerate into rituals that have lost their meaning. Or how a tradition in the church that may have once been full of meaning for us can become a ritual that no longer is a means of obedience to God.

Question 9. Remember that the religious leaders condemned their Lord and Creator when they condemned Jesus. They rejected God after having personal encounters with him that no one in history had ever experienced!

Question 11. He expresses a longing for them. In sending the prophets, wise men and teachers, he had given them many opportunities to repent.

Study 18. Matthew 24. The Return of the King.

Purpose: To consider the importance of living in perseverance and the need to live in anticipation of the King's return.

General note. This chapter has been abused and misused. People who want a blueprint for the future miss the primary focus and value of Christ's words. Jesus clearly indicates that everything in heaven and earth will pass away—except those who are related to him, who believe and obey his Word. One of the reasons that the chapter is misused so greatly is because much of it is difficult to understand. It will not be possible to explore the depth of this passage, nor many of the issues it raises. Keep in mind that the central focus is the return of Christ. Now that Jesus has condemned the religious leaders and they have determined to kill him, Jesus must prepare the disciples for his final victory on the cross and his return for heaven.

Question 1. The temple represented the presence of God. As long as the temple was standing, every Israelite believed that God was present with his people. Especially since the exile and the return, the nation of Israel had become increasingly fanatical about the temple and the system rituals associated with it. The temple—along with keeping the sabbath and food purity laws, all of which Jesus attacked—became a source of idolatry.

Question 2. The key to understanding this chapter is keeping in mind the questions asked by the disciples: When will the temple be destroyed and what will be the sign of your coming and the end of the age?

Question 3. Wars, earthquakes and famines are not the signs of his coming. They have happened throughout history.

Question 5. It is not clear when the abomination that causes desolation will take place. Commentators differ on whether this took place in A.D. 70 or whether it is to take place in the future just prior to Christ's second coming. The early Christians understood it to refer to their time and fled Jerusalem prior to its destruction by the Romans. Some believe it has a double meaning and was given both for the early Christians and for those who will be living at the time of Christ's return.

Question 6. Many commentators believe the events referred to in verses 15-25 focus primarily on the fall of Jerusalem at the hands of the Romans in A.D. 70. But it is possible that Jesus had more than just the Roman conquest in mind.

Question 9. Jesus' return will be visible to all. Throughout history, some have advocated a secret return of Jesus to a specially selected group. Others have suggested that Jesus has returned by means of another incarnation. However, Jesus is coming back as the same person, with a resurrected body, and this will be known to all. In some way his return will have to do with the skies. Lightning can be seen by anyone looking at the sky. Likewise, vultures and celestial bodies can be seen by anyone looking at the sky.

Study 19. Matthew 25. Preparation for the King's Return.

Purpose: To consider the ways that Jesus holds us accountable for our actions until he returns.

Question 1. Now that Jesus has told the disciples that he is leaving them for a while, he tells them how they must live until he returns. The thrust of the parables is that we must live in constant expectation and in consistent obedience.

Question 2. The point of the parable of the ten virgins is that Jesus wants us to be prepared and to live in anticipation of his return. Don't be sidetracked by a discussion of eternal security.

Question 6. Sometimes this parable is used to justify a conservative use of church money in the name of stewardship. It appears that Jesus expects investments that have an element of risk. The genuine disciple of Jesus is responsible for the resources given to him or her. Jesus did not judge people for the amount of return but for the lack of initiative and investment.

Question 7. The lazy servant falsely views the master as hard and unjust. Or at least he offers this view in order to justify his lack of initiative. Jesus, using to the principle of "according to your faith," uses this servant's explanation as the standard of judgment.

Question 9. It is common to interpret the parable of the sheep and goats simply in terms of the hungry, the sick and those in prison. In this view entrance into the kingdom will be solely on the basis of the treatment of the poor and oppressed. Some have even claimed that the parable abolishes all distinctions between Christians and non-Christians since anyone who is benevolent will gain access into the kingdom. The proper interpretation of the parable hinges on not only the treatment of the sheep and goats but also the identity of Jesus' "brothers." It is very possible that Jesus' brothers refer to his disciples (see especially 12:48-49; 28:10; 23:8). The fate of the nations will be determined by how they respond to Jesus' followers—those who are charged with spreading the gospel and do so in the face of hunger, thirst, illness and imprisonment. Good deeds done to Jesus' followers, even the least of them, are not only works of compassion and morality but reflect where people stand in relation to the kingdom and Jesus himself.

Study 20. Matthew 26. The Betrayal of the King.

Purpose: To see how the treacherous trial of the King is his triumph and our failure.

General note. The plot against Jesus is consummated in chapters 26 and 27. In this study we see Jesus submit to the schemes of religious leaders for the sake of his mission. There is a wide variety of actions and emotions. There are the terrible treachery of Judas and the tender compassion of Mary, the touching intimacy of the Last Supper and painful apathy of Gethsemane, the passion of Jesus in the garden and the resigned passiveness of Jesus at his trial.

Question 1. Ever since Jesus' birth, when Herod tried to destroy him with the unwitting guidance of the religious leaders, he has been in mortal danger. As it will become clear to the apostles and the early church, Jesus was born to die. The decision by the religious leaders, now very purposeful, and the anointing of Jesus' feet set the stage for the final events for Jesus' impending death.

Question 2. The atmosphere is both ominous and hopeful. It is ominous because Jesus is speaking of his death. It is hopeful because he speaks of drinking with them again in the kingdom. How confused the disciples must have been!

Question 3. The allusion to the Passover in the Old Testament is unmistakable. The celebration of the Passover and the covenant at Mt. Sinai were the center of worship in the Old Testament. Now Jesus is himself becoming the Passover lamb and making a new covenant. In this meal we have the creation of the new people of God, and this meal is the embodiment of all that Jesus has done and will do.

Question 5. Jesus is no Socrates who goes stoically to his death because it was determined by fate. He is fully human, with a desire and will of his own. Death is terrible, and he does not want to die. In addition, the spiritual dynamics of death for him are worse than for any other human. Not only does he experience a break in his fellowship with his heavenly Father, but he will take on the entire weight of human sin. Nothing could be worse, and he does not look forward to it. We miss the great deed that Jesus has done for us if we take lightly that Jesus died because it was God's will for him to do so. And Jesus, of course, always did what God wanted him to do.

Question 6. The ability to do what is right is always an exercise in spiritual power. In the climactic events that the disciples are involved in there are dark spiritual forces coming against them. Only by means of prayer could there be any hope of having the strength to stay with Jesus and choose to support him.

Question 7. In verses 15-16 Judas makes himself available; he can be bought. Yet strangely his actions are part of the divine plan.

Question 9. The appeal to Scripture for what was happening to Jesus would have made him seem a religious fanatic for those who were already opposed to him. To his followers it would have added a sense of divine presence and purpose.

Question 10. There are at least three reasons for Jesus' silence: his mission is to die, his accusers are not interested in the truth, and the attempt to defend himself would imply that his accusers had the authority to judge him. Jesus has maintained all along that he, not they, was the rightful source of judgment and authority in Israel.

Question 11. The initial effect of Jesus' statement is to make the chief priest furious. However, the ultimate effect will be that Jesus, as judge of the world, will be the final judge of his accusers. Jesus is alluding to Daniel 7:14, when the Son of Man will come at the end of the age to judge everyone.

Question 12. Peter believes in Jesus, so he wants to be near Jesus in his distress. His fear of death, however, is stronger than his faith at this point in his life. As was mentioned in the note on the disciples in the Garden of Gethsemane, it takes spiritual power to choose to resist temptation, and the disciples had not prayed earlier to exercise that power.

Study 21. Matthew 27. The Crucifixion of the King.

Purpose: To consider the mysterious triumph of the kingdom of heaven through the suffering and death of Jesus on the cross.

General note. This is a grim chapter. Jesus is killed. It appears that evil will triumph. Both the international authorities (the Romans) and the local authorities (the Jewish leaders) participate in Jesus' death. You may discover that there is a sense of defeat as you finish the study. This is to be expected. We all need to look at the terrible reality of the death of Jesus. After you finish the study, encourage people to look forward to the last chapter, the resurrection.

Question 1. The powerlessness of the religious leaders is displayed in these verses. Due to the occupation by Rome, they did not have the right to execute him. They had to find away to convince Pilate, the Roman governor, to carry out their death sentence.

Question 2. Jesus has set these events up by his words and actions, especially during the last week of confrontation after he assaulted the temple. Now things are unfolding according to his plan.

The early Christians would look back at Jesus' behavior on this night and see a fulfillment of Isaiah 53:7, "He was oppressed and afflicted, yet he did not open his mouth; he was led like a lamb to the slaughter, and as a sheep before her shearers is silent, so he did not open his mouth."

Question 4. The charges against Jesus don't appear to be clear. It appears from Pilate's question and Jesus' answer about being king of the Jews that the religious leaders were accusing Jesus of leading a rebellion against Rome. This was obviously false for at least two reasons. First, Jesus had not raised an army to resist the Romans. Second, why would the Jewish leaders, who hated being occupied by Rome, be so concerned about a rebellion that they would capture Jesus and turn him over for being a revolutionary?

Question 5. If Jesus defended himself to Pilate, it would be an acknowledgment that the Roman legal system had authority over him. Jesus however, believes that he, not the Romans, is the legitimate authority over all the nations. He does not defend himself, but merely affirms that he is indeed King of the Jews.

Question 7. It was obvious that Jesus' message had gotten through and people knew what he taught. Those who mocked him demonstrated that they just did not believe him. Jesus was mocked for saying he was king, that he could raise up the temple of God, that he was the Son of God and that he had come to save Israel. If he died (and stayed dead) then obviously all these statements were indeed false and Jesus would be shown to be a fake.

Question 8. There is a split in the Godhead that had effects through all creation. Jesus is quoting Psalm 22:1, which says, "My God, my God, why have you forsaken me? Why are you so far from saving me, so far from the words of my groaning?"

Question 10. Most of Jesus' followers were not present. However, the women watched from a distance. Joseph showed courage in asking for the body of Jesus. Some of the emotions they might have felt were sadness, responsibility, loyalty, love, care and pain.

Study 22. Matthew 28. The Victory of the King.

Purpose: To consider how the resurrection of Christ is the victory that his disciples can't keep quiet about.

General note. The mystery of the kingdom of heaven that has been confusing to the disciples takes on new clarity as Jesus returns from the grave. While Jesus physically leaves them, he becomes more present than ever as he ascends to heaven. Upon the foundation of Jesus' life, death and resurrection, the disciples can truly become fishers of people, as he promised.

Question 1. Throughout the book of Matthew everything happens in response to Jesus. If we have eyes to see it, everything in the world and in our lives also happens in response to Jesus.

Question 3. The women were prepared by the ministry of Jesus to cope with the angelic presence. The guards were not and so, ironically, they become "as dead" in place of the one who they thought was dead.

Question 4. Throughout the book of Matthew, from the appearance of angels at his birth to angels at his death, there is a dynamic that one needs supernatural preparation in order to understand Jesus.

Question 5. Jesus only makes sense when there is preparation for him. We have to know something about ourselves and something about why he is coming before we can take in just who he is and what is expected of us.

Question 7. The religious leaders have been given the final sign promised them in Matthew 16:1ff, the sign of Jonah. Jesus has been in the grave and has risen. But as has been evident all along, the religious leaders are not open to the work of God and are only interested in preserving their power.

Question 8. How would the disciples have gotten by the Roman guards in order to steal the body? The penalty for sleeping on duty was death. Even if the guard did fall asleep, how would the disciples get past a sleeping guard and move the large gravestone that blocked the cave without waking the guards?

Question 9. Jesus promised at the transfiguration that there were some standing there who would not taste death until they saw the kingdom of heaven come with power. Now that Jesus stands before them, that promise has been fulfilled. Peter, James and John got a glimpse of the transfiguration. Now all the disciples see Jesus transformed. Before his resurrection he told the disciples to keep his transformation a secret. Now he tells them to spread the word through the world.

Question 10. When the birth of Jesus was promised to Mary, he was called Immanuel, God with us. As the Gospel of Matthew ends, that is what Jesus affirms. By his spiritual ascent to heaven he also becomes spiritually united with his people in all places and all times. The conclusion of the Gospel is the same as it was at the beginning, "the kingdom of heaven is at hand, repent and believe the good news." Hearing this, the disciples with Jewish ears would have struggled to get outside of their nationalism. They thought the Messiah was just for the Jews. With our modern ears we tend to hear that Christians should tell others what to believe. Jesus is tells us to tell people all over the world his message so that they may enter his kingdom.

Question 12. An important element of the Great Commission is that the disciples were to teach whatever he commands. In effect the Gospel of Matthew becomes the discipling manual of the early church. Perhaps it should be the discipling manual of the modern church as well!

Stephen Eyre is pastor for ministry support and Christian discipleship at College Hill Presbyterian Church in Cincinnati, Ohio. He has authored the LifeGuide® Bible Studies Christian Beliefs *and* Deuteronomy. *Jacalyn Eyre has extensive experience leading Bible studies.*